THE *Lyric* LIBRARY

Contemporary Christian

Complete Lyrics for 200 Songs

HAL•LEONARD®

Other books in *The Lyric Library*:

Broadway Volume I

Broadway Volume II

Christmas

Classic Rock

Country

Early Rock 'n' Roll

Love Songs

Pop/Rock Ballads

ISBN 0-634-04353-6

Library of Congress cataloguing-in-publication data has been applied for.

Visit Hal Leonard Online at
www.halleonard.com

Preface

The expression of religious devotion and spiritual praise by means of song is a tradition as old and deep-rooted as the practice of religion itself. From its inception at the dawn of our Common Era, the Christian faith has embraced this musical form of sacred celebration as a way of conveying scriptural message, divine adoration, and the experience of personal redemption. The earliest incarnations of this practice served as an essential supplement to religious service; the musical arrangement and lyrical content of such hymns were composed largely for Sunday-only articulation within consecrated space.

But life in the twenty-first century brings with it challenges, circumstances, and lifestyles neither experienced nor anticipated by the early Christian songwriters. So as not to lose resonance with the modern, workaday world, today's hymnodists interpret Christianity's most time-honored and cherished beliefs with contemporary significance, incorporating into its long-standing ideals the impressions and imagery readily identifiable to a contemporary audience.

Now, these modernized adaptations of the Christian perspective have been thoughtfully selected and brought together in the *Contemporary Christian* edition of *The Lyric Library*, a compilation of lyrics to 200 of the most essential, contemporary Christian songs, complete in one convenient volume. With each lyric presented in poetic form, this devotional anthology is integral to every Christian literature collection. Whether its content serves as a guide in sing-alongs; is reviewed for clarification of unknown, forgotten, or misheard lyrics; or is simply perused in quiet contemplation, the *Contemporary Christian* lyric book is one that will be read time and time again.

With a repertoire that covers a wide variety of musical genres—country, rock, adult contemporary, pop—and compositions written and performed by some of today's most-loved artists and groups—Amy Grant, Michael W. Smith, Steven Curtis Chapman, Twila Paris, Delirious?, DC Talk, ZOEgirl—the *Contemporary Christian* lyric book reflects the growing popularity of Christian songwriting within the prevailing musical sphere.

As relevant to the contemporary songwriting fan as to the devout follower of the Christian faith, these verses of worship, joy, compassion, awe, gratitude, love, and enlightenment are sure to appeal to and inspire those who partake of this modern-day world.

Contents

Contemporary Christian

Abba (Father)

Words and Music by Rebecca St. James, Tedd Tjornhom and Otto Price

recorded by Rebecca St. James

I'm feeling like the eagle that rises,
Flies above the earth and its troubles.
Oh, yes, he knows that there are
    valleys below,
But under his wings there's a
    stronger power.

Oh, Father, You are my strength.
On You I wait upon.

Refrain:
You make the road rise up to meet me.
You make the sunshine warm upon my face.
The wind is at my back and the rain
    falls soft.
God, I lift You high.
You are my Abba.

Running in this race 'til the finish line,
The only road for me is the narrow.
Not gonna stop or even look to the side
When I fix my eyes on You, Jesus.

Oh, Father, You are my strength,
Now more than ever.

Refrain Twice

When you run too far,
(And the road is long,)
Can't walk another mile,
(He is waiting,)
Hope in Him again.
(He'll renew you.)
Gather up your wings and fly.

Refrain Twice

Do you not know?
Have you not heard?
He gives strength to the weary,
To those who hope in Him.
They will soar like eagles.

Adonai

Words and Music by Lorraine Ferro, Don Koch and Stephanie Lewis

recorded by Avalon

One single drop of rain,
Your salty tears became blue ocean;
One tiny grain of sand turning in Your hand,
A world in motion.

You're out beyond the furthest morning star;
Close enough to hold me in Your arms.

Refrain:
Adonai,
I lift up my heart and I cry.
My Adonai,
You are Maker of each moment,
Father of my hope and freedom;
Oh, my Adonai.

One timid, faithful knock
Resounds upon the Rock of Ages;
One trembling heart and soul
Becomes a servant bold and courageous.

You call across the mountains and the seas;
I answer from the deepest part of me.

Refrain

From age to age You reign in majesty,
And today You're making miracles in me.

Refrain

After the Rain

Words and Music by Connie Harrington, Joe Beck and Neal Coomer

recorded by Aaron•Jeoffrey

I cover my heart, turn from the wind,
Button my coat;
Here comes the storm again.
What can I do but to trust in Him?

'Cause I know the deeper my faith runs,
The stronger I become.
And the thunder, it may shake me,
But I always know that

Refrain 1:
After the rain you can look to the sky again;
The clouds will give way to the light of
   the sun.
After the rain,
You know that you've made it through,
And you'll fin'lly see the joy from the pain;
After the rain.

Ev'ryone needs, ev'ryone hurts,
Ev'ryone feels the weight of the
   world sometimes,
But don't let the wind sweep your heart away.

'Cause even the roughest waters cleanse,
So when they come again,
Let them serve as a reminder
You can always know that

Refrain 1

Can't you see the hand of Jesus reaching
   out for you?
You never have to face the storm alone.

Refrain 1

Refrain 2:
You know that you made it,
You know that you made it.
Light of the sun.
You know you made it,
You know you made it,
So hold on, hold on
After the rain.

Refrain 2

Always Have, Always Will

Words and Music by Grant Cunningham, Toby McKeehan and Nick Gonzales

recorded by Avalon

Part of me is the prodigal,
Part of me is the other brother.
But I think the heart of me is really some-
    where between them.
Some days I'm running wild,
Some days we're reconciled.
But I wonder all the while why You put up
    with me,
When I wrestle most days to find ways to
    do as I please.

Refrain:
I always have.
I always will.
You saved me once.
You save me still.
A longing heart Your love alone can fill.
You always have, oh.

Always will.

Spoken:
You always have.
You always will.

I was born with a wayward heart;
Still I live with the restless spirit.
My soul is so well worn you'd think I'd
    have arrived by now.

I'm caught in the trappings of my search
    for a lasting love.
I've made mistakes enough to last me
    a lifetime.
Still slip, I still fall.
But I'll always run back to You.

Refrain

Always will.

I'm gonna keep trusting You.
I see what You've seen me through.
I'm goin' where You have gone.
I'm letting You lead me,
I'm letting You lead me home.

All my days,
Always, and forever.
Never far,
Never leave me, never.
Here I'll stay.
Ever love me, ever.
Here's my heart.
I'll always love You.
Love you, yeah, yeah.

Refrain Twice

Oh, you always will.
You always will.

Angels

Words and Music by Amy Grant, Gary Chapman, Michael W. Smith and Brown Bannister

recorded by Amy Grant

"Take this man to prison,"
The man heard Herod say,
And then four squads of soldiers came
And carried him away.

Chained up between two watchmen,
Peter tried to sleep,
But beyond the walls an endless pray'r
Was lifting for his keep.

Then a light cut through the darkness
Of a lonely prison cell,
And the chains that bound the man of God
Just opened up and fell,

And running to his people
Before the break of day,
There was only one thing on his mind,
Only one thing to say:

Refrain:
Angels watching over me,
Ev'ry move I make.
Angels watching over me.
Angels watching over me,
Ev'ry step I take,
Angels watching over me.

God only knows the times my life
Was threatened just today,
Reckless car ran out of gas
Before it ran my way.

Near misses all around me,
Accidents unknown,
Though I never see with human eyes
The hands that lead me home.

But I know they're all around me,
All day and through the night,
When the enemy is closing in
I know sometimes they fight

To keep my feet from falling,
I'll never turn away,
If you're asking what's protecting me,
Then you're gonna hear me say:
Got His—

Refrain

Angels watching over me,
Angels watching over me.
Got His—

Refrain

Angels watching over me,
Angels watching over me,
Angels watching over me,
Angels watching over me.
Though I never see with human eyes,
The hands that lead me home.

Another Time, Another Place

Words and Music by Gary Driskell

recorded by Sandi Patty & Wayne Watson

I've always heard there is a land
Beyond the mortal dreams of man,
Where ev'ry tear will be left behind,
But it must be in another time.

Oh, there'll be an everlasting light
Shining a purest holy white.
And ev'ry fear will be erased,
But it must be in another place.
Oh, oh,

Refrain:
So I'm waiting for another time and another place,
Where all my hopes and dreams
Will be captured with one look at Jesus' face.
Oh, my heart's been burnin',
My soul keeps yearnin'
Sometimes I can't hardly wait
For that sweet, sweet someday,
When I'll be swept away to another time and another place.

I've grown so tired of earthly things,
They promise peace but furnish pain.
All of life's sweetest joys combined
Could never match those in another time.

Oh, and though I've put my trust in Christ,
And felt His Spirit move in my life,
I know it's truly just a taste
Of His glory in another place.
Oh, oh—

Refrain Twice

Anything Is Possible

Words and Music by Chrissy Conway, Alisa Girard, Kristin Swinford and Joe Priolo

recorded by ZOEgirl

I know that you've been thinking;
I see it in your eyes.
You're holding on to something,
But still you don't know why.

So walk by faith and not by what you see.
Trust your heart and let yourself believe.

Refrain 1:
I can do things,
Things you never knew,
Change your world,
Make it all brand new.
I can do miracles if you want me to.
Anything is possible for you.

Refrain 2:
Anything, anything, anything,
Anything is possible.
Anything, anything, anything,
Anything is possible.

I know your heart's been broken,
You feel so all alone,
But I will never leave you lonely,
I'll never let you go.

So walk by faith and not by what you see.
It's up to you to let your heart believe.

Refrain 1

If I can make the heavens,
If I can make a rain,
If I can make your heart beat,
Then I can ease your pain.

If I'm the only answer,
The only one that's right,
Why are you still searching?
Why do you still fight?
When—

Refrain 1

Refrain 2

Refrain 1 Twice

Arise, My Love

Words and Music by Eddie Carswell

recorded by Newsong

Not a word was heard at the tomb that day,
Just shuffling soldiers' feet as they guarded
    the grave.
One day, two days, three days had passed.
Could it be that Jesus breathed His last?

Could it be that His Father has forsaken Him,
Turned His back on His Son, despising
    our sin?
All hell seemed to whisper, "Just forget Him,
    He's dead!"
Then the Father looked down to his Son
    and said,

Refrain:
"Arise, my love,
Arise, my love;
The grave no longer has a hold on You.
No more death's sting,
No more suffering.

Arise, arise, my love."

The earth trembled and the tomb began
    to shake,
And like lightning from heaven the stone
    rolled away.
And as dead men, the guards stood there
    in fright
As the power of love displayed its might.

Then suddenly a melody filled the air;
Riding wings of wind, it was ev'rywhere.
The words all creation had been longing
    to hear,
The sweet sound of vict'ry so loud and clear:

Refrain

Arise, arise!

Sin, where are your shackles?
Death, where is your sting?
Hell has been defeated;
The grave could not hold the King!

Refrain

Arise, arise, arise!

Arms of Love

Words and Music by Amy Grant, Michael W. Smith and Gary Chapman

recorded by Amy Grant

Lord, I'm really glad You're here.
I hope You feel the same when You see all my fear,
And how I've failed.
I fall sometimes.

It's hard to walk in shifting sand.
I miss the rock and find I've nowhere left to stand,
And start to cry.

Lord, please help me raise my hands,
So You can pick me up.
Hold me close, hold me tighter.
I have found a place where I can hide,

Refrain:
It's safe inside Your arms of love.
Like a child who's held throughout a storm,
You keep me warm in Your arms of love.

Storms will come and storms will go;
I wonder just how many storms it takes until
I fin'lly know.
You're here always.

Even when my skies are far from gray,
I can stay, teach me to stay
There in the place I found where I can hide,

Refrain

Awesome God

Words and Music by Rich Mullins

recorded by Rich Mullins

When He rolls up His sleeve, He ain't just "puttin' on the Ritz."
Our God is an awesome God!
There is thunder in His footsteps and lightnin' in His fist.
Our God is an awesome God!

And the Lord wasn't jokin' when He kicked 'em out of Eden;
It wasn't for no reason that He shed His blood.
His return is very close and so you better be believin'
That our God is an awesome God!

Refrain:
Our God is an awesome God;
He reigns from heaven above.
With wisdom, pow'r and love,
Our God is an awesome God!

Refrain

And when the sky was starless
In the void of the night,
Our God is an awesome God!
He spoke into the darkness
And created the light.
Our God is an awesome God!

The judgment and wrath He poured out on Sodom,
The mercy and grace He gave us at the cross.
I hope that we have not too quickly forgotten
That our God is an awesome God!

Refrain Twice

Our God is an awesome God!
Our God is an awesome God!

The Basics of Life

Words and Music by Don Koch and Mark Harris

recorded by 4HIM

We've turned the page, for a new day
   has dawned,
And we've rearranged what is right and
   what's wrong,
Somehow we've drifted so far from the truth
That we can't get back home.

And where are the virtues that once gave
   us light,
And where are the morals that governed
   our lives?
Someday we all will awake and look back
At just to find what we've lost.

Refrain:
We need to get back to the basics of life,
A heart that is pure and a love that is blind;
A faith that is fervently grounded in Christ,
The hope that endures for all time.
These are the basics,
We need to get back to the basics of life.

The newest rage is to reason it out,
And just meditating you can overcome
   any doubt;
After all, man is a god,
They say God is no longer alive.

But I still believe in the old rugged cross,
Woo, I still believe there is hope for the lost.
And I know the Rock of all ages
Will stand through the changes of time,
Through the changes of time.

Refrain

We've let the darkness invade us too long,
We gotta turn the tide.
Oh, and we need the passion that burned
   long ago,
To come and open our eyes,
There's no room for compromise!

We need to get back to the basics of life,
A heart that is pure and a love that is blind!

Refrain Twice

Basics of life.
Basics of life.

Between You and Me

Words and Music by Toby McKeehan and Mark Heimermann

recorded by DC Talk

Sorrow is a lonely feeling,
Unsettled is a painful place.
I've lived with both for far too long now
Since we've parted ways.
I've been wrestling with my conscience
And I found myself to blame.
If there's to be any resolution
I've got to peel my pride away.

Refrain:
Just between you and me I've got something
  to say,
Wanna get it straight before the sun goes
  down.
Just between you and me confession needs
  to be made,
Recompense is my way to freedom now.

Just between you and me I've got something
  to say.

If confession is the road to healing,
Forgiveness is the promised land,
I'm reaching out in my conviction,
I'm longing to make amends.
So, I'm sorry for the words I've spoken,
For I've betrayed a friend.
We've got a love that's worth preserving
And a bond I will defend.

Refrain

Just between you and me I've got something
  to say.

In my pursuit of God,
I thirst for holiness,
As I approach the Son,
I must consider this.

Offenses unresolved,
They'll keep me from the throne.
Before I go to Him my wrong
Must be atoned.

If there's to be any resolution,
I've got to peel this pride away.

Refrain Twice

It's my way to freedom.
I've got something to say,
So let me say it today.
I've got something to say,
Confession needs to be made.
I've got something to say,
Confession needs to be made.
I've got something to say.

Beyond Belief

Words and Music by Bob Hartman

recorded by Petra

We're content to pitch our tent
When the glory's evident.
Seldom do we know the glory came and went.

Moving can seem dangerous
In this stranger's pilgrimage.
Knowing that you can't stand still, you cross the bridge.

Refrain:
There's a higher place to go,
Beyond belief, beyond belief.
Where we reach the next plateau,
Beyond belief, beyond belief.
And from faith to faith we grow,
T'wards the center of the flow
Where He beckons us to go,
Beyond belief, beyond belief.

Leap of faith without a net
Makes us want to hedge our bet.
Waters never part until our feet get wet.

There's a deeper place to go
Where the road seems hard to hoe.
He who has begun this work won't let it go,
Let it go.

Refrain

And it takes so long to see the change.
But we look around and it seems so strange.
We have come so far but the journey's long.
And we once were weak but now we're strong.

Refrain

Big House

Words and Music by Audio Adrenaline

recorded by Audio Adrenaline

I don't know where you lay your head,
Or where you call your home.
I don't know where you eat your meals
Or where you talk on the phone.
I don't know if you got a cook,
A butler, or a maid.
I don't know if you got a yard
With a hammock in the shade.

I don't know if you got some shelter,
Say a place to hide.
I don't know if you live with friends
In whom you can confide.
I don't know if you got a fam'ly,
Say a mom or a dad.
I don't know if you feel love at all
But I bet you wish you had.

Come and go with me to my father's house.
Come and go with me to my father's house.

Refrain:
It's a big, big house with lots and lots
of room.
A big, big table with lots and lots of food.
A big, big yard where we can play football.
A big, big house.
It's my father's house.

Ib-i-dib-i-dee-bop-bop-bow, Whew! Yeah!

All I know is a big ol' house
With rooms for ev'ryone.
All I know is alots of land
Where we can play and run.
All I know is that you need love
And I've got a family.
All I know is you're all alone,
So why not come with me?

Come and go with me to my father's house.
Come and go with me to my father's house.

Refrain Twice

My father's house.

Come and go with me to my father's house.
Come and go with me to my father's house.

Refrain Twice

Breathe on Me

Words and Music by Grant Cunningham and Matt Huesmann

recorded by Sandi Patty

Breathe on me, breath of God;
Bring my life close to Your Spirit.
Beat in me, heart of God;
My soul's in prayer to be near it.

Focus my eyes to only see what's You.
And breathe on me,
Breathe on me breath of God.

Breathe on me, breath of God;
I am a vessel to be filled.
Comfort me, peace of God;
Lord, I am restless for Your will.

Silence my fears, silence my fears,
So that I may hear from You.
And breathe on me,
Breathe on me breath of God.

Surround me in Your glory,
Make Your presence known.
Set the path of grace before me,
Let Your breath become my own.

Breathe on me, breath of God;
Cover my sin with Your mercy.
Speak to me, Word of God;
Give me a light for my journey.

Show me Your way,
Show me Your way,
And draw me close to You.
And breathe on me,
Breathe on me,
Breathe on me breath of God.

Can't Live a Day

Words and Music by Connie Harrington, Joe Beck and Ty Lacy

recorded by Avalon

I could live life alone
And never fill the longings of my heart,
The healing warmth of someone's arms.

And I could live without dreams,
And never know the thrill of what could be
With ev'ry star so far and out of reach.

I could live without many things and I could
   carry on,
But—

Refrain:
I couldn't face my life tomorrow
Without Your hope in my heart.
I know I can't live a day without You.
Lord, there's no night and there's no
   morning
Without Your loving arms to hold me.
You're the heartbeat of all I do.

I can't live a day without You.

And oh, I could travel the world,
See all the wonders beautiful and new.
They'd only make me think of You.

And I could have all life offered,
Riches that were far beyond compare,
To grant my ev'ry wish without a care.

Oh, I could do anything, oh, yes.
But if You weren't in it all,

Refrain

I can't live a day without You.

Oh, Jesus,
I live because You live.
You're like the air I breathe.
Oh, Jesus,
Oh, I have because You gave.
You're everything to me.
Oh—

Refrain Twice

The Change

Words and Music by Steven Curtis Chapman and James Isaac Elliott

recorded by Steven Curtis Chapman

Well, I got myself a tee shirt that says what I believe.
I've got letters on my bracelet to serve as my I.D.
I've got the necklace and a key chain
And almost ev'rything a good Christian needs.

I've got the little proverb magnet on my refrigerator door,
And a welcome mat to bless you before you walk across my floor.
I got a Jesus bumper sticker
And the outline of a fish stuck on my car.

And even though this stuff's all well and good,
I cannot help but ask myself,

Refrain:
What about the change?
And what about the diff'rence?
What about the grace?
And what about forgiveness?

And what about a life that's showing I'm undergoing the change?
Yeah, I'm undergoing the change.

Well, I've got this way of thinking;
It comes so nat'rally.
Well I believe the whole world is revolving around me.
And I've got this way of living that I have to die to ev'ry single day,

'Cause if God's Spirit lives inside of me,
I'm gonna live life diff'rently:

I'm gonna have the change;
I'm gonna have the diff'rence,
I'm gonna have the grace;
I'm gonna have forgiveness.

I'm gonna live a life that's showing I'm undergoing the change.

Spoken:
Therefore, if anyone is in Christ, he is a new creation.
Therefore, if anyone is in Christ, he is a new creation.
The old has gone and the new has come

Refrain

I wanna live a life that's showing I'm undergoing the change.

What about the diff'rence?
What about the grace?
And what about forgiveness?
I wanna live a life that's showing I'm undergoing the change.

What about the change?
What about the change?
What about the change?

Spoken:
Lord change me.

Circle of Friends

Words and Music by Douglas McKelvey and Steve Siler

recorded by Point of Grace

We were made to love and be loved,
But the price this world demands will cost you far too much.
I spent so many lonely years just trying to fit in.
Now I've found a place in this circle of friends.

Refrain:
In a circle of friends,
We have one Father.
In a circle of friends,
We share this prayer:

That ev'ry orphaned soul will know,
And all will enter in to the shelter of this circle of friends.

If you weep, I will weep with you.
If you sing for joy, the rest of us will lift our voices too.
But no matter what you feel inside, there's no need to pretend.
That's the way it is in this circle of friends.

Refrain

That we'll gather together,
No matter how the highway bends.
I will not lose this circle of friends.

Among the nations, tribes, and tongues,
We have sisters and brothers.
And when we meet in heaven,
We will recognize each other.

Joy so deep, and love so sweet.
Oh, we'll celebrate these friends and a life that never ends.

Refrain

That it will not be long before
All will enter in to the shelter of this circle of friends.
That it will not be long before
All will enter in to the shelter of this circle of friends.

Repeat to End:
Circle of friends.

Colored People

Words and Music by Toby McKeehan and George Cocchini

recorded by DC Talk

Refrain 1:
(One one one one two two two two
Three three three three four four four four)

Pardon me, your epidermis is showing, sir.
I couldn't help but note your shade of melanin.
I tip my hat to the colorful arrangement,
'Cause I see the beauty in the tones of our skin.

We've gotta come together and thank the Maker of us all.

Refrain 2:
We're colored people,
And we live in a tainted place.
We're colored people,
And they call us the human race.
We've got a history so full of mistakes,
'Cause we are colored people who depend
On a Holy Grace.

Refrain 1

A piece of canvas is only the beginning,
For it takes on character with ev'ry loving stroke.
This thing of beauty is the passion of an Artist's heart.
By God's design we are a skin kaleidoscope.

We've gotta come together, aren't we all human after all?

Refrain 2

Ignorance has wronged some races,
And vengeance is the Lord's.
If we aspire to share this space,
Repentance is the cure.

Refrain 1

Well, just a day in the shoes of a colorblind man
Should make it easy for you to see
That these diverse tones do more than cover our bones
As a part of our anatomy.

Refrain 2

We're colored people,
And they call us the human race.
Ooh, oh, colored people.
We're colored people,
And we all gotta share this space.
Yeah, we've got to come together somehow.

We're colored people,
And we live in a tainted world.
Red, yellow, black and white.
We're colored people, every man, woman, boy, and girl.
Colored people, colored people,
Colored people, colored people, yeah.

The Coloring Song

Words and Music by Dave Eden

recorded by Petra

Red is the color of the blood that flowed
Down the face of someone who loved us so.
He's the perfect Man, He's the Lord's own Son,
He's the Lamb of God, He's the only One
That can give us life, that can make us grow,
That can make the love between us flow.

Blue is the color of a heart so cold
That will not bend when the story's told
Of the love of God for a sinful race,
Of the blood that flowed down Jesus' face
That can give us life, that can make us grow,
That can keep our hearts from growing cold.

Gold is the color of the morning sun
That shines so freely on ev'ryone.
It's the sun of love that keeps us warm,
It's the sun of love that calms the storm,
That can give us life, that can make us grow,
That can turn our mornings into gold.

Brown is the color of the autumn leaves
When the winter comes to the barren trees.
There is birth, there is death, there is a plan
And there's just one God, and there's just one Man
That can give us life, that can make us grow,
That can make our sins as white as snow.

That can give us life, that can make us grow,
That can turn our mornings into gold.
That can give us life, that can make us grow,
That can keep our hearts from growing cold.
That can give us life, that can make us grow,
That can make the love between us flow.

Consume Me

Words and Music by Toby McKeehan, Michael Tait, Kevin Max and Mark Heimermann

recorded by DC Talk

Na na na…

Lovely traces,
I can sense You in ev'rything.
The way that You move me takes me
    far away,
I seek no escape.

I'm dreaming through Your eyes,
I am wand'ring through Your mind.
I'm overtaken by the way that You
    deliver me,
I'm transcended.
There's no place I'd rather be than here
    in Heaven.
Without You I'm incomplete,
It's hopeless.

Refrain 1:
You consume me,
You consume me,
Like a burning flame running through
    my veins.

Refrain 2:
You consume me,
Moving through me.
Anytime, anyplace, You invade my space.
You consume me,

You consume me.

Wholly devoted, I immerse myself in You.
Baptize me in Your love.
'Cause drowning in the thought of You floods
    my soul;
I'm taken by the things You do,
God, You know it doesn't matter what I lose,
I'm Yours.

Refrain 1

You consume me.

I am in Your hands, under Your command,
Like a puppet on a string.
So You know I am willing to put my faith
    in You,
So before the world I sing.
You consume me,
You consume me.

(Burning flame through my veins.)

Refrain 2

Oh, You know that I surrender.
I am consumed, I'm consumed with You.

There's no other way I can fly.
It's You and I, You and I.
There's no other way I can fly.
It's You and I, You and I.

Could He Be the Messiah

Words and Music by Deborah D. Smith and Michael W. Smith

recorded by Michael W. Smith

Been here for days, I'm amazed
At this teacher, carpenter, preacher.
Lost in the crowd, I hear Him now,
He's praying, and He's saying,
God feed them all.

Five thousand men, all of His friends
Are worried: find bread and hurry!
Five loaves and fish what can He wish
He's praying, still He's saying,
God feed them all.

Refrain:
Could He be the Messiah,
Miracle Man,
Part of the plan?
Could He be the Messiah,
Life in His hand?
I understand He could be.

Bread for our needs, fully He feeds
Our hunger, older and younger.
Twelve baskets more can we ignore,
He shows us that He knows us;
Is He the Christ?

God in His eyes, I realize
His power, need of the hour.
Jesus His name, they say He came
To feed us and to receive us;
Is He the Christ?

Refrain Twice

It is He, the Messiah,
Miracle man,
Part of the plan.
It is He, the Messiah,
Life in hand,
I understand it is He!

THE LYRIC LIBRARY

Creed (Credo)

Words and Music by David "Beaker" Strasser

recorded by Rich Mullins

Verse 1:
I believe in God the Father, Almighty Maker
Of Heaven and Maker of Earth, and in
 Jesus Christ,
His only begotten Son, Our Lord.

He was conceived by the Holy Spirit,
Born of the Virgin Mary,
Suffered under Pontius Pilot,
He was crucified, dead and buried.

Refrain:
And I believe what I believe is what makes
 me what I am.
I did not make it,
No, it is making me;

It is the very truth of God and not the
 invention of any man.

I believe that He who suffered
Was crucified, buried, and dead.
He descended into Hell
And on the third day rose again.

He ascended into Heaven
Where He sits at God's mighty right hand.
I believe that He's returning
To judge the quick and the dead of the
 sons of men.

Refrain

It is the very truth of God and not the invention of any man.
And—

I believe it, I believe it.
I believe it.
I believe, I believe it.

Repeat Verse 1

I believe in the Holy Spirit, one Holy Church,
The communion of Saints, the forgiveness
 of sin.
I believe in the resurrection, I believe in
 life that never ends.

Refrain

I did not make it,
No, it is making me.
I said, I did not make it,
No, it is making me;
It is the very truth of God,
Not the invention of any man.

Repeat Eleven Times:
I believe it.

Cross of Gold

Words and Music by Michael W. Smith and Wayne Kirkpatrick

recorded by Michael W. Smith

Where do you stand?
What is your statement?
What is it you're trying to say?
What's in your hand?
What's in your basement?
What's in the cards you don't play?

Are you holding the key,
Or are you intending to pick the lock of
    heaven's gate?
It's confusing to me,
The message you're sending,
And I don't know if I can relate,
Oh—

Refrain:
What's your line?
Tell me why you wear your cross of gold.
State of mind,
Or does it find a way into your soul?

Is it a flame?
Is it a passion, a symbol of love living in you?
Or is it a game,
A religion in fashion,
Some kind of phase you're going through?

We all travel the extremes
From cellar to rafter, looking for a place in
    the sun.
So, I'm trying to see
What you're headed after,
But I don't know where you're coming from,
Oh—

Refrain

What's your line?
Tell me why you wear that cross of gold.

Spoken:
For some, it's simply something to wear
    around your neck,
Just a trinket of jewelry.
Is it decoration or proclamation, an icon
    of what?
For some, it's simply something to wear
    around your neck.
It means a lot more than that to me.

Refrain Twice and Fade

Deeper

Words and Music by Martin Smith and Stuart Garrard

recorded by Delirious?

I want to go deeper,
But I don't know how to swim.
I want to be meeker,
But have you seen this old earth?
I want to fly higher,
But these arms won't take me there.
I want to be, I want to be.

Refrain 1:
And maybe I could run and maybe I
    could fly to You.
And do You feel the same
When all You see is blame in me?
Hey!

Refrain 2:
And the wonder of it all is that I'm living
    just to fall
More in love with You.
And the wonder of it all is that I'm living
    just to fall

More in love with You, yeah.

I want to go deeper,
But is it just a stupid whim?
I want to be weaker,
Be a help to the strong.
I want to run faster,
But this old leg won't carry me.
I want to be, I want to be.

Refrain 1

Refrain 2

More in love with You, yeah.

Refrain 2

Maybe I could run, maybe I could follow.
It's time to walk the path where many seem
    to fall.

Hold me in Your arms,
Just like any father would.
How long do we have to wait?
How long?
We're going all the way.
Hey!

Refrain 2

More in love with You, yeah.
The wonder of it all.

Refrain 2

More in love with You.

Destined to Win

Words and Music by Ed DeGarmo and Dana Key

recorded by DeGarmo & Key

This song's to all the people with the light in their hearts
And love in their eyes.
You don't have to worry when the mountains seem
Of infinite size.

There is One who goes before you to calm the sea.
There's a King who leads His people to victory!

Refrain:
We are destined to win!
We're surrounded by His love,
Guarded by His power!
Destined to win!
Following the Lord until the battle's over,
We are destined to win!

We all get discouraged when the pressures of life
Start weighing us down.
We've learned that, in His footsteps, crosses in life
Must precede the crown.

There is One who goes before you to calm the sea.
There's a King who leads His people to victory!

Refrain

We've got to remember it's our destiny
To win in the end.
With Christ on our side, we are destined to win!

Refrain

We are destined,
We are destined to win!

Dive

Words and Music by Steven Curtis Chapman

recorded by Steven Curtis Chapman

The long awaited rains
Have fallen hard upon the thirsty ground;
They've carved their way
To where the wild and rushing river can
    be found.
And like the rain I have been carried here
To where the river flows, yeah.

My heart is racing
And my knees are weak as I walk to
    the edge.
I know there is no turning back
A-once my feet have left the ledge.
And in the rush, I hear a voice that's
    telling me
It's time to take the leap of faith,
So here I go.

Refrain:
I'm diving in;
I'm going deep, in over my head.
I wanna be caught in the rush,
Lost in the flow.
In over my head I wanna go.
The river's deep;
The river's wide;
The river's water is alive,
So sink or swim, I'm diving in.

There is a supernatural power
In this mighty river's flow.
It can bring the dead to life
And it can fill an empty soul
And give our heart the only thing worth living
And worth dying for, yeah.

But we will never know
The awesome power of the grace of God
Until we let ourselves get swept away
Into this holy flood.
So if you take my hand, we'll close our eyes
    and count to three
And take the leap of faith.
Come on, let's go.

Refrain

I'm diving in.
Oh, I'm diving in, yeah.
I'm diving in, yeah, here I go.
Come on, let's go.

Refrain Twice

So sink or swim, I'm diving in.
So sink or swim, I'm diving in.
I'm diving in.

I'm diving in, I'm going deep,
In over my head I wanna be, I'm diving in.
I'm diving in, I'm going deep,
In over my head I wanna be, I'm diving in.

Don't Look at Me

Words and Music by Stacie Orrico and Mark Heimermann

recorded by Stacie Orrico

Refrain 1:
Don't look at me if you're lookin' for
   perfection.
Don't look at me; I will only let you down.

Refrain 2:
I'll do my best to point you in the right
   direction,
But don't look at me, no, no, no,
Don't look at me;

Look at Him.

Sometimes I have a fear that you will see a
   mirror
And get the thought that it's the main
   attraction.
But all that you detect is just what I reflect
Of the object of my own affection.

I'll lead you to the One I found;
He'll give you ev'rything you need.

Refrain 1

Refrain 2

Look at Him.

It's understandable to want a hero,
But people can't meet all your expectations.
Still, some can teach you things about the
   love He brings;
Just know the source of life is in the Savior.

I'll lead you to the One I found;
He'll give you ev'rything you need.

Refrain 1

Refrain 2

He's the One who lived a perfect life;
He's the One who always gets it right.
He's the One and only guiding light;
Oh, yeah.

He's ev'rything you want to be;
He's the answer to your ev'ry need.
If you follow Him, then you will see
He's like no other, yeah.

Refrain 2

Don't look at me.

Refrain 2

Look at Him.

Don't Worry

Words and Music by Rebecca St. James and Matt Bronleewe

recorded by Rebecca St. James

On the corner of Fifth and Broadway,
I was walking to the grocery store.
On Third, I saw a man upon a box
And he seemed a little unorthodox.
Well, he was preaching up a storm,
And as I walked on by he said:

Refrain:
"Don't worry about your life,
'Cause if you hold it too close you'll lose it.
Don't worry about your life,
So won't you let go before it's gone?"

A little further on I saw a beggar on
    the street.
He asked for change, then gives me his
    life story.
Well, he said he was a millionaire
But he made some bad decisions there,
And now a dollar-fifty could feed him for
    a week.
And he said—

Refrain

The I see the birds, I watch them fly.
They got ev'rything they need.
They show me why I can be free,
Knowing You will care for me.

Well, fin'lly at the grocery store,
My mind is filled with many thoughts
As I bump into a girl I knew from
    high school.
She said, "What's diff'rent about you, girl?"
And I smiled and said, "This is what I
    know is true,
And I'll pass it right along to you."

Refrain Twice and Fade

Doubly Good to You

Words and Music by Richard Mullins

recorded by Amy Grant

If you see the moon rising gently on your fields,
If the wind blows softly on your face,
If the sunset lingers while cathedral bells peal,
And the moon has risen to her place,

Refrain:
You can thank the Father
For the things that He has done,
And thank Him for the things He's yet to do.
And if you find a love that's tender,
If you find someone who's true,
Thank the Lord,
He's been doubly good to you.

And if you look in the mirror at the end of a hard day,
And you know in your heart you have not lied.
And if you gave love freely, if you earned an honest wage,
And if you've got Jesus by your side,

Refrain Twice

Thank the Lord,
He's been doubly good to you.

Down on My Knees

Words and Music by Wayne Kirkpatrick

recorded by Susan Ashton

I've got a witness not too stable.
It wouldn't get me very far.
I've got one hand on the table
And one in the cookie jar.
I've got sins that need eviction
From a temple that's a wreck.
I've got a chain of contradiction
Hanging around my neck.

So, I go down, I go down, down,
I go down on my knees.

I feel the bitter winds grow colder,
They are dancing with my pride.
I've got a chip on my shoulder
Bigger than a mountain side.
And these claws of human nature
Hold me tight within their clasp.
I'm not worthy of forgiveness,
But I just have to ask.

So, I go down, I go down, down,
I go down on my knees.

Refrain:
Feed the hunger, slake my thirst
For a spiritual rebirth.
Light my darkness, move in me.
Make me more than what you see
As I go down on my knees.

When I've all but killed the fire
And my soul's in desp'rate need
But I wallow in the mire of complacency,
That's when I go down on my knees.

Yeah, I want to taste the fruit I'm missing,
And yet I feast only on the bread.
My desire's alive and kicking,
But my drive is dead.
So, I go down on my knees.

Refrain

You bear the weight of condemnation,
Cleansing with the blood of truth.
So, with my humble acclamation
I want to give myself to You.

Repeat Twice:
So, I go down, I go down, down,
I go down on my knees.

Each One, Reach One

Words and Music by Babbie Mason

recorded by Babbie Mason

Today a man is somewhere, proclaiming the good news,
Winning families to Jesus, all around his neighborhood.
He tells them that God is able to make their house a home.
He wants to win his world for Christ, but he can't do it alone.
But—

Refrain:
Each one can reach one.
As we follow after Christ, we all can lead one.
We can lead one to the Savior.
Then together we can tell the world that Jesus is the way,
If we each one, reach one.

The message is unchanging: "Go ye into all the world
And share the love of Jesus," far away or door-to-door.
Just like somebody told you that Jesus loves you so,
You must tell someone who will tell someone,
Until the whole world knows.
For—

Refrain

So will you go and labor?
Will you hold high your light?
One by one, and two by two,
We can win our world for Jesus Christ.
For—

Refrain

El Shaddai

Words and Music by Michael Card and John Thompson

recorded by Amy Grant; Michael Card

Refrain 1:
El Shaddai, El Shaddai,
El Elyon na Adonai,
Age to age You're still the same,
By the power of the name.

Refrain 2:
El Shaddai, El Shaddai,
Er kamkana Adonai,
We will praise and lift You high,
El Shaddai.

Through Your love and through the ram,
You saved the son of Abraham.
Through the power of Your hand,
You turned the sea into dry land.
To the outcast on her knees,
You were the God who really sees,
And by Your might You set your
    children free.

Refrain 1

Refrain 2

Through the years You made it clear
That the time of Christ was near,
Though the people couldn't see
What Messiah ought to be.
Though Your Word contained the plan,
They just could not understand;
Your most awesome work was done
In the frailty of Your Son.

Refrain 1

Refrain 3:
El Shaddai, El Shaddai,
Er kamkana Adonai,
I will praise You till I die,
El Shaddai.

Refrain 1

Refrain 3

Every Heart That Is Breaking

Words and Music by Twila Paris

recorded by Twila Paris

For the young abandoned husband
Left alone without a reason,
For the pilgrim in the city where there is no home.
For the son without a father,
For his solitary mother,
I have a message:

He sees you, He knows you, He loves you,
He loves you.

Refrain:
Ev'ry heart that is breaking tonight is the heart of a child
That he holds in His sight;
And oh, how He longs to hold in His arms
Ev'ry heart that is breaking tonight.
Ev'ry heart that is breaking tonight.

For ev'ry heart.

For the precious, fallen daughter,
For her devastated father, for the prodigal who's dying
In a strange new way.
For the child who's always hungry,
For the patr'ot without a country,
I have a message:

He sees you, He knows you, He loves you,
Jesus loves you.

Refrain

Ev'ry heart that is breaking tonight.
For ev'ry heart.

Every Season

Words and Music by Nichole Nordeman

recorded by Nichole Nordeman

Ev'ry evening sky,
An invitation to trace the patterned stars.
And early in July,
A celebration for freedom that is ours.
And I notice You in children's games,
In those who watch them from the shade.
Ev'ry drop of sun is full of fun and wonder.
You are summer.

And even when the trees
Have just surrendered
To the harvest time, forfeiting their leaves
In late September and sending us inside.
Still I notice You when the change begins
And I am braced for colder winds,
I will offer thanks for what has been and what's to come.
You are autumn.

And ev'rything in time
And under heaven fin'lly falls asleep.
Wrapped in blankets white,
All creation shivers underneath.
And still I notice You when the branches crack
And in my breath on frosted glass.
Even now in death, You open doors for life to enter.
You are winter.

And ev'rything that's new
Has bravely surfaced, teaching us to breathe.
And what was frozen through
Is newly purposed, turning all things green.
So it is with You and how You make me new
With ev'ry season's change.
And so it will be as You are recreating me,
Summer, autumn, winter, spring.

Everything

Words and Music by Martin Smith

recorded by Delirious?

It's a beautiful day, and the world is bright,
'Cause You took me away from the longest night.
What can I do
But give all I have to You.

It's a beautiful day, and the page has turned.
Deep in my soul now Your fire burns.
What can I do?
I'll give it all up for—

Refrain:
You give me ev'rything,
Give me hope to win,
You're the song I sing.
You give me ev'rything,
Give me hope to win,
You're the song I sing.

It's a beautiful day, and we're running proud.
And we'll run to the line, hear the witness crowd.
I know it's true, we're gonna fly,
We're gonna dance on that glorious day
With—

Refrain

You give me ev'rything,
Give me hope to win,
You're the song I sing.
You're the song I sing, yeah.

Repeat Three Times:
You are the light that shines.

Faithful Friend

Words and Music by Twila Paris and Steven Curtis Chapman

recorded by Twila Paris & Steven Curtis Chapman

Ev'ryone knows you as a man of honor.
I am glad to know you simply as a friend.
You've always taken time to be my brother,
And I'll be standing by you in the end.

But I will never put you on a pedestal.
I thank the Lord for ev'rything you do.
I'll be there to pray for you,
And for the ones you love.
I believe that He will finish all He started
   in you.

Refrain:
I will be an open door that you can
   count on;
Anywhere you are, anywhere you've been.
I will be an honest heart you can depend on.
I will be a faithful friend.

I am one of many whose path has been
   made clearer
By the light you've carried faithfully
As a warrior and a child.
God has used you greatly to encourage
   and inspire.
And you've remained a true friend all
   the while.

So I will never put you on a pedestal,
'Cause we both know all the glory is
   the Lord's.
And I'll be there to pray
That He will keep you by His grace.
And I will always remind you to be
   seeking His face.

Refrain

Should it ever come your time to mourn,
I will weep with you.
And ev'ry single time you win,
I'm celebrating too.
I will celebrate with you.

Refrain

I will, I will be faithful.
I will be a faithful friend.

Father's Eyes

Words and Music by Gary Chapman

recorded by Amy Grant

I may not be ev'ry mother's dream for her
  little girl,
And my face may not grace the mind of
  ev'ryone in the world.
But that's alright as long as I can have one
  wish I pray,
When people look inside my life, I want to
  hear them say:

She's got her Father's eyes,
Her Father's eyes,
Eyes that find the good in things
When good is not around,
Eyes that find the source of help
When help just can't be found,

Refrain:
Eyes full of compassion,
Seeing ev'ry pain,
Knowin' what you're goin' through
And feelin' it the same.
Just like my Father's eyes,
My Father's eyes,
My Father's eyes,
Just like my Father's eyes.

On that day when we will pay for all the
  deeds we have done,
Good and bad, they'll all be had to see by
  everyone.
And when you're called to stand and tell just
  what you saw in me,
More than anything I know, I want your
  words to be:

She had her Father's eyes,
Her Father's eyes,
Eyes that found the good in things
When good was not around,
Eyes that found the source of help
When help would not be found,

Refrain

My Father's eyes.
My Father's eyes.
Just like my Father's eyes.

Favorite Song of All

Words and Music by Dan Dean

recorded by Phillips, Craig & Dean; The Brooklyn Tabernacle Choir

He loves to hear the wind sing
As it whistles through the pines on
   mountain peaks
And He loves to hear the raindrops
As they splash to the ground in a magic
   melody.
He smiles in sweet approval
As the waves crash to the rocks in harmony.
Creation joins in unity
To sing to Him majestic symphonies.
But—

Refrain:
His fav'rite song of all is the song of the
   redeemed
When lost sinners now made clean
Lift their voices loud and strong;
When those purchased by His blood
Lift to Him a song of love.
There's nothing more He'd rather hear,
Nor so pleasing to His ear
As his fav'rite song of all.

And He loves to hear the angels
As they sing, "Holy, holy is the Lamb."
Heaven's choirs in harmony
Lift up praises to the great "I Am."
But He lifts His hands for silence
When the weakest saved by grace begins
to sing
And a million angels listen
As a newborn soul sings "I have been
   redeemed."

'Cause—

Refrain

It's not just melodies and harmonies
That catches His attention.
It's not just clever lines and phrases
That causes Him to stop and listen

But when any heart set free,
Washed and bought by Calvary,
Begins to sing.
That's—

Refrain

Repeat Twice:
Holy, holy, holy is the Lamb.
Hallelujah, Hallelujah.

© 1992 DAWN TREADER MUSIC
Admin. by EMI CHRISTIAN MUSIC PUBLISHING

Find a Way

Words and Music by Michael W. Smith and Amy Grant

recorded by Amy Grant

You tell me your friends are distant,
You tell me your man's untrue.
You tell me that you've been walked on,
And how you feel abused.
So you stand here an angry young woman,
Taking all the pain to heart.
I hear you saying you want to see changes,
But you don't know how to start.

Refrain:
Love will find a way.
(How do you know?)
Love will find a way.
(How can you see?)
I know it's hard to see the past
And still believe
Love is gonna find a way.
(I know that—)
Love will find a way.
(A way to go.)
Love can make a way.
(Only love can know.)
Leave behind the doubt,
Love's the only out.
Love will surely find a way.

I know this life is a strange thing,
I can't answer all the why's.
Tragedy always finds me
Taken again by surprise.
I could stand here an angry young woman,
Taking all the pain to heart.
But I know that love can bring changes,
And so we've got to move on.

Refrain

If our God, His Son not sparing,
Came to rescue you,
Is there any circumstance
That He can't see you through?

Refrain and Fade

Fool for You

Words and Music by Nichole Nordeman

recorded by Nichole Nordeman

There are times when faith
And common sense do not align,
When hardcore evidence
Of You is hard to find.
And I am silenced in the face
Of argumentative debate
And it's a long hill, it's a lonely climb.
'Cause they want proof.

They want proof of all these mysteries I
    claim,
'Cause only fools would want to chant a
    dead man's name.
Maybe it's true, yeah.

Refrain:
I would be a fool for You.
All because You asked me to.
A simpleton who's seemingly naïve.
I do believe
You came and made Yourself a fool for me.

I admit that in my darkest hours
I've asked "What if?"
What if we created some kind
Of manmade faith like this?
Out of good intention
Or emotional invention
And after life is through
There will be no You.

'Cause they want proof of all these miracles
    I claim,
'Cause only fools believe that men can walk
    on waves.
Maybe it's true, yeah.

Refrain

Unaware of popularity,
Unconcerned with dignity,
You made me free.
That's proof enough for me.

I would be a fool for You.
Only if You asked me to.
A simpleton who's only thinking of the cause
    of love.
I will speak Jesus' name.
If that makes me crazy, they can call me
    crazed.
I'm happy to be seemingly naïve.
I do believe
You came and made Yourself a fool for me.
Ah, a fool for You.

For Such a Time as This

Words and Music by Wayne Watson

recorded by Wayne Watson

Now, all I have is now to be faithful,
To be holy and to shine,
Lighting up the darkness.
Right now, I really have no choice
But to voice the truth to the nations;
A generation looking for God.

Refrain:
For such a time as this
I was placed upon the earth,
To hear the voice of God and do His will,
Whatever it is.
For such a time as this,
For now and all the days He gives.
I am here, I am here, and I am His
For such a time as this.

You, do you ever wonder why,
Seems like the grass is always greener
Under ev'rybody else's sky?
But right here, right here for this time and place,
You can live a mirror of His mercy,
A forgiven image of grace.

Can't change what's happened till now,
But we can change what will be
By living in holiness,
That the world will see Jesus.

Refrain Twice

For Who He Really Is

Words and Music by Steven Curtis Chapman and Geoff Moore

recorded by Steven Curtis Chapman

"Too many hypocrites," I heard her say.
"I even saw it in the headlines today.
How can I follow God when His own people
    turn away?

Nobody's perfect but I just want to see
Somebody living what they say they believe.
If they've got all this world needs like
    they say,
I wonder why won't they give some away."

Can she see God for who He really is
In what she sees in you and me?
Yeah, can she see God for who He really is?
For who He really is
Is all she really needs to see.

He slips into church and he puts up
    his guard.
They look so happy but his life's been
    so hard.
He keeps his distance so they won't see
    the scars.

It's just religion that's all dressed up
    in white,
And God is love as long as you're living right.
But does he know that Jesus also had scars,
And His love can reach him no matter
    how far?

Can he see God for who He really is
In what he sees in you and me?
Yeah, can he see God for who He really is?
For who He really is
Is all he really needs to see.
All he really needs to see.

The skeptics are watching to see who
    will fall,
While those disillusioned search for the
    truth in it all.

Maybe today we'll cross their paths unaware
And they'll stop and look at us.
What will be there?

Can they see God for who He really is
In what they see in you and me?
Yeah, can they see God for who He really is?
For who He really is
Is all they really need to see.
All they really need to see.

Can they see God and who He really is?
We really need to see who He really is.
We really need to see who He really is.

Friend of a Wounded Heart

Words and Music by Wayne Watson and Claire Cloninger

recorded by Wayne Watson

Smile, make 'em think you're happy,
Lie and say that things are fine.
And hide that empty longing that you feel,
Don't ever show it.
Just keep your heart concealed.

Why are the days so lonely?
I wonder where, where can the heart go
    free?
And who will dry the tears that no one's
    seen?
There must be someone to share your silent
    dreams.

Caught like a leaf in the wind, lookin' for a
    friend,
Where can you turn?
Whisper the words of a prayer and you'll
    find Him there,
Arms open wide, love in His eyes.

Refrain:
Jesus, He meets you where you are.
Oh, Jesus, He heals your secret scars.
All the love you're longing for is Jesus,
The Friend of a wounded heart.

Joy comes like the mornin';
And hope deepens as you grow.
And peace beyond the reaches of your soul
Comes flowin' in through you,
For love has made you whole.

Once like a leaf in the wind, lookin' for a
    friend,
Where could you turn?
You spoke the words of a prayer and you
    found Him there,
Arms open wide, love in His eyes.

Refrain

Oh, Jesus,
He heals your secret scars.
All the love you're longing for,
All the love that you need,
Oh, is Jesus,
The Friend of a wounded heart.

Repeat and Fade:
Oh, the Friend of a wounded heart.

Friends

Words and Music by Michael W. Smith and Deborah D. Smith

recorded by Michael W. Smith with Amy Grant

Packing up the dreams God planted
In the fertile soil of you;
Can't believe the hopes he's granted
Means a chapter in your life is through.

Refrain 1:
But we'll keep you close as always;
It won't even seem you've gone,
'Cause our hearts in big and small ways
Will keep the love that keeps us strong.

Refrain 2:
And friends are friends forever
If the Lord's the Lord of them.
And a friend will not say "never"
'Cause the welcome will not end.
Though it's hard to let you go,
In the Father's hands we know
That lifetime's not too long
To live as friends.

With the faith and love God's given
Springing from the hope we know,
We will pray the joy you'll live in
Is the strength that now you show.

Refrain 1

Refrain 2 Twice

No, a lifetime's not too long
To live as friends.

Give It Away

Words and Music by Michael W. Smith, Amy Grant and Wayne Kirkpatrick

recorded by Michael W. Smith

She asked him for forever and a promise that would last.
He said, "Babe, you know I love you,
But I can't commit to that."
She said, "Love isn't love till you give it away."

A father lived in silence, saw his son become a man.
There was a distance felt between them,
'Cause he could not understand
That love isn't love till you give it away.

Refrain:
You gotta give it away.
As we live,
Moving side by side,
May we learn to give,
Learn to sacrifice.

We can entertain compassion for a world in need of care.
But the road of good intentions doesn't lead to anywhere,
'Cause love isn't love till you give it away.

Refrain

Love is like a river flowing down from the giver of life.
We drink from the water and our thirst is no longer
Denied.
Ooh—

Refrain

There was a man who walked on water,
He came to set the people free.
He was the ultimate example of what love can truly be,
'Cause His love was His life and He gave it away.

Refrain Twice

Go and Sin No More

Words and Music by Rebecca St. James, Tedd Tjornhom and Michael Anderson

recorded by Rebecca St. James

I've sinned, come on my knees,
For I'm not worthy of your love.
How could You die for me?
Such grace can only come from God.
Oh Lord, You search and You know me.
You see me inside out.
God, You alone can forgive me,
Erase my fear and my doubt.

Refrain 1:
Father, You pick me up.
I feel like a child in Your arms.
I don't deserve this love,
But I hear Your voice, Lord Jesus.

Refrain 2:
"Go and sin no more."
He said, "I will not condemn you.
I'll forgive and forget it all.
Go and sin no more.
My child, let Me remind you,
It is I who'll lead and guide you as you go."

You are my purpose.
You are the reason that I live.
I want to be like You.
Help me to love and to forgive.
God, let me not be distracted.
Lord, help me focus on You.
Keep sin from ruling my life, Lord.
Make me holy and pure.

Refrains 1 and 2

Wipe, wipe away.
Take, take away.
Break, break away.
Fill my life; make it right.
Father, help me,
Father, help me go.

Refrain 2

He said, "I will not condemn you, no.
Go and sin no more.
My child, let Me remind you,
It is I who'll lead and guide you as you go!"

Refrain 3:
I've sinned, come on my knees.
How could you die for me?
You search my heart, know my thoughts,
See me inside out
And all throughout me.
You alone can forgive me.
You always pick me up,
Like a child in Your arms.
I could stay with You forever here.

Refrain 3 and Fade

Go Light Your World

Words and Music by Chris Rice

recorded by Kathy Troccoli

There is a candle in ev'ry soul;
Some brightly burning, some dark and cold.
There is a Spirit who brings a fire,
Ignites a candle and makes His home.

So, carry your candle,
Run to the darkness,
Seek out the hopeless,
Confused and torn.
Hold out your candle for all to see it.
Take your candle and go light your world.
Take your candle and go light your world.

Frustrated brother, see how he's tried
To light his own candle some other way.
See now your sister, she's been robbed
    and lied to,
Still holds a candle without a flame.

So, carry your candle,
Run to the darkness,
Seek out the lonely,
The tired and worn.
Hold out your candle for all to see it.
Take your candle and go light your world.
Take your candle and go light your world.

We are a fam'ly whose hearts are blazing,
So let's raise our candles and light up
    the sky.
Praying to our Father, in the name of Jesus,
Make us a beacon in the darkest time.

So, carry your candle,
Run to the darkness,
Seek out the helpless,
Deceived and poor.
Hold out your candle for all to see it.
Take your candle and go light your world.
Take your candle and go light your world.

God

Words and Music by Rebecca St. James and Tedd Tjornhom

recorded by Rebecca St. James

He made the night, He made the day,
Spread the earth upon the waters,
Made the heavens and the rain.
Look at the sky, see its design,
The very same Creator
Is the One who gave us life.

And what is man that He's mindful of us?
We're merely clay in His hands.
And what am I that He loves me so much
  He would die?
You know, all I can say is it's—

Refrain:
God, truly God.
Can you see, can you hear,
Can you touch, can you feel?
It's God, truly God.
I can't explain any other way
'Cuz it's

God.

Inside us all, there is a void.
All mankind is searching
For the one who fills the soul.
In Him there's hope.
In Him there's life.
The world cries for a savior that's right
  before their eyes.

And what is man that He takes us in
As His children to be His own?
And what are we that he wants to be our
  Father?
All that I can say is it's—

Refrain Twice

God.

Lord, I praise You for Your endless love,
Your boundless grace.
I stand here amazed.

God, truly God.
I can't explain any other way
'Cuz it's—

Refrain

God, truly God.
It's God, truly God.

God Is God

Words and Music by Steven Curtis Chapman

recorded by Steven Curtis Chapman

And the pain falls like a curtain
On the things I once called certain,
And I have to say the words I fear the most:
"I just don't know."
And the questions without answers
Come and paralyze the dancer,
So I stand here on the stage afraid to move,
Afraid to fall.

Oh, but fall I must
On this truth: that my life has been formed
    from the dust.

Refrain:
God is God and I am not.
I can only see a part of the picture
    He's painting.
God is God and I am man,
So I'll never understand it all,
For only God is God.

And the sky begins to thunder,
And I'm filled with awe and wonder,
'Til the only burning question that
    remains is,
"Who am I?"
Can I form a single mountain?
Take the stars in hand and count them?
Can I even take a breath
Without God giving it to me?

He is first and last
Before all that has been, beyond all that
    will pass.

Refrain

Great is the Lord; holy, holy, great is
    the Lord.
Great is the Lord; holy, holy, great is
    the Lord.

Oh, how great are the riches of His wisdom
    and knowledge,
How unsearchable, for to Him and
    through Him
And from Him are all things.

So let us worship before the throne of
    the One
Who is worthy of worship alone.
Oh, God—

Refrain

Only God is God.

Repeat and Fade:
Great is the Lord; holy, holy, great is
    the Lord.

God Is in Control

Words and Music by Twila Paris

recorded by Twila Paris

This is no time for fear.
This is a time for faith and determination.
Don't lose the visions here, carried away by
 the motion.
Hold on to all that you hide in your heart.
There is one thing that has always been true.
It holds the world together.

Refrain:
God is in control.
We believe that His children will not be
 forsaken.
God is in control.
We will choose to remember and never
 be shaken.
There is no power above or beside Him.
We know, oh, God is in control.
Oh, God is in control.

History marches on.
There is a bottom line drawn across the
 ages.
Culture can make its plan, but the line never
 changes.
No matter how the deception may fly,
There is one thing that has always been true.
It will be true forever.

Refrain

He has never let you down.
Why start to worry now?
Why start to worry now?
He is still the Lord of all we see
And He is still the loving Father,
Watching over you and me.

Watching over you, watching over me.
Watching over ev'rything.
Watching over you, watching over me.
Ev'ry little sparrow, ev'ry little king.
Oh, ev'ry little king.

Refrain

Oh, God is in control.
Oh, God is in control.

God of All of Me

Words by Bob Farrell
Music by Michael W. Smith

recorded by Sandi Patty

Lord, You are God of the morning light,
Master of the shining sun and Ruler of the night;
God of the earth and God of the sea,
Voice that fills creation from the mountains' majesty.
Lord God of all, You know my ways.
Giver of breath to my dying day.

Almighty God of all I can see,
Build up Your kingdom in me.

Refrain:
Father, take my heart,
Hold it in Your hand,
Be the God of all of me.
Father, take my life,
Ev'rything I am;
Keeper of my soul,
God of all of me.

Lord, in my soul, in secret parts of me,
There are places in my heart that only You can reach.
Brighter shines my hope than the morning light;
Deeper is my stain of sin than any dark of night.
Father who rules all of earth and sea,
Reign over dreams that I dare not speak.

Lord God of all, be God of these.
Rule ev'ry kingdom in me.

Refrain Twice

Keeper of my soul, God of all of me.
Keeper of my soul, God of all of me.

God So Loved

Words and Music by Chris Eaton

recorded by Jaci Velasquez

Ba ba ba ba ba…

Refrain
God so loved the world
That He gave His one and only Son,
That whosoever believes in Him will not perish
But have everlasting life.

I try so hard to find the words to say,
To let you know how great is this God to whom I pray.
Nothing can or ever will compare
To the peace that flows in your soul when He is living there.

Oh, I know you've been through so much,
It's hard to contemplate letting go and reaching out in trust.
But I know the simple truth that love is here for you.
So take Him at His word and see what He can do.

Refrain

The promise is yours and mine;
Take hold of this love for the rest of your life.

Ba ba ba ba ba…

But it's time to take a step of faith.
Be prepared for Jesus' love to carry you away.

Refrain

Repeat Four Times:
God so loved the world.

God You Are My God

Words and Music by Stuart Garrard

recorded by Delirious?

God, You're my God, You're my God.
God, You're my God, You're my God.

And I will seek You; yes, I will seek You.
And I will seek You; yes, I will seek You.

You satisfy my soul.
You satisfy my soul.

So I praise You as long as I live.
So I praise You as long as I live.

I've seen You're power and You're glory,
You've let me see You in the sanctuary.
Because Your love is better than my life,
I'll lift up my hands in sacrifice.

We give You praise, give You praise.
We give You praise.
We give You praise, give You praise.

For You are worthy.
For You are worthy, yes, You are worthy.
Yes, You are worthy, yes, You are worthy.
So I will praise You as long as I live.
So I will praise You.
I will praise You as long as I live, yeah.

God's Own Fool

Words and Music by Michael Card

recorded by Michael Card

It seems I've imagined Him all of my life
As the wisest of all of mankind;
But if God's holy wisdom is foolish to men,
He must have seemed out of His mind.
For even His family said He was mad
And the priests said, "A demon's to blame;"
But God in the form of this angry young man
Could not have seemed perfectly sane.

Refrain 1:
When we in our foolishness thought we were wise,
He played the fool and he opened our eyes.
When we in our weakness believed we were strong,
He became helpless to show were wrong.
And—

Refrain 2:
So we follow God's own fool;
For only the foolish can tell.
Believe the unbelievable;
Come be a fool as well.

So come lose your life for a carpenter's son,
For a madman who died for a dream.
Then you'll have the faith His first followers had,
And you'll feel the weight of the beam.
So surrender the hunger to say you must know,
Have the courage to say: "I believe."
For the power of paradox opens your eyes,
And blinds those who say they can see.

Refrains 1 and 2

Refrain 2

God's Romance

Words and Music by Martin Smith

recorded by Delirious?

There's a song that ev'ryone can sing,
There's a prayer that ev'ryone can bring.
Feel the music, 'cause it's time to dance.
People all across the world
With a heartbeat for holiness
Feel His pleasure, we are God's romance.

Hear the sound; let it shake the ground.
Now's the time for the saints to shine.

Refrain:
Ev'ryone, here is the Kingdom, come.
Here is the God who saves the day.
And we will gladly run
Into the glorious Son
Singing that Jesus is Alive.

There's a song that ev'ryone can sing,
There's a race that ev'ryone can win.
Leave your sadness, it's our time to dance.
Ev'ryone let out your praise,
People with their hearts ablaze.
We've found Jesus, He's our great romance.

Hear the sound; let it shake the ground.
Now's the time for the saints to shine.

Refrain

It's time to shine, it's time to shine.

Repeat Four Times:
Holy is the Lord.

Refrain

Grand Canyon

Words and Music by Wayne Kirkpatrick

recorded by Susan Ashton

I've seen You calm the waters raging
In the rivers of my mind.
Your Spirit it blows a breeze into my soul.
And I've felt the fire that warms the heart,
Knowing that it comes from You.
Then I've let it turn as cold as a stone.
Oh—

Refrain:
Sometimes I feel like I'm as close as Your shadow.
Sometimes I feel like I'm looking up at You
From the bottom of the Grand Canyon,
So small and so far,
From the Grand Canyon with a hole in my heart.
And I'm a long way from where I know I need to be
When there's a grand canyon in between You and me.

I've had the faith that gave me strength
For moving any mountainside.
I've felt the solid ground beneath my feet.
But I've had the bread of idleness
While drinking from a well of doubt,
And it shakes the core of all I believe.
Oh—

Refrain

There's a grand canyon between You and me.

Refrain

When there's a grand, grand canyon between You and me.

The Great Adventure

Words and Music by Steven Curtis Chapman and Geoff Moore

recorded by Steven Curtis Chapman

Saddle up your horses.

Started out this morning in the usual way,
Chasing thoughts inside my head of all I had to do today.
Another time around the circle,
Try to make it better than the last.

I opened the Bible and I read about me.
Said I'd been a pris'ner and God's grace had set me free.
And somewhere between the pages it hit me like a lightning bolt.
I saw a big frontier in front of me, and I heard somebody say,
"Let's go!"

Refrain:
Saddle up your horses!
We've got a trail to blaze
Through the wild blue yonder of God's amazing grace.
Let's follow our leader into the glorious unknown.
This is life like no other.
This is the great adventure.
Yeah.

Come on, get ready for the ride of your life.
Gonna leave long-faced religion in a cloud of dust behind
And discover all the new horizons just waiting to be explored.
This is what we were created for,

Refrain

We'll travel over, over mountains so high.
We'll go through valleys below.
Still through it all,
We'll find that this is the greatest journey
That the human heart will ever see.
The love of God will take us far beyond our wildest dreams.

Oh, saddle up your horses!
Come on, get ready to ride.

Refrain

Repeat and Fade:
Come on!
This is the great adventure.

The Great Divide

Words and Music by Matt Huesmann and Grant Cunningham

recorded by Point of Grace

Silence, trying to fathom the distance,
Looking out 'cross the canyon carved by my hands.
God is gracious.
Sin would still separate us
Were it not for the bridge His grace has made us.
His love will carry me.

Refrain:
There's a bridge to cross the great divide,
A way was made to reach the other side.
The mercy of the Father cost His Son His life.
His love is deep, His love is wide.
There's a cross to bridge the great divide.

God is faithful.
On my own I'm unable.
He found me hopeless, alone and sent a Savior.
He's provided a path and promised to guide us
Safely past all the sin that would divide us.
His love delivers me.

Refrain

The cross that cost my Lord His life has given me mine.

There's a bridge to cross the great divide.
There's a cross to bridge the great divide.

Refrain

There's a cross to bridge the great divide.

Great Is the Lord

Words and Music by Michael W. Smith and Deborah D. Smith

recorded by Michael W. Smith

Refrain:
Great is the Lord.
He is holy and just,
By the power we trust His love.
Great is the Lord, He is faithful and true,
By His mercy He proves He is love.

Great is the Lord, and worthy of glory,
Great is the Lord, and worthy of praise.

Great is the Lord, now lift up your voice,
Now lift up your voice: Great is the Lord!
Great is the Lord!

Refrain

Great is the Lord, and worthy of glory,
Great is the Lord, and worthy of praise.

Great are You, Lord, I lift up my voice,
I lift up my voice: Great are You, Lord!
Great are You, Lord!

Great is the Lord, and worthy of glory,
Great is the Lord, and worthy of praise.

Great are You, Lord, I lift up my voice,
I lift up my voice: Great are You, Lord!
Great are You, Lord!

Great are You, Lord!
Great are You, Lord!
Great are You, Lord!

He Walked a Mile

Words and Music by Dan Muckala

recorded by Clay Crosse

Before the threads of time began,
Was preordained a mighty plan
That I should walk with Him alone,
The cords of trust unbroken.
But fate foresaw my wand'ring eye
That none could yet restrain;
To violate the friendship,
I would cause Him so much pain.

Refrain:
And ev'ry time I close my eyes,
I see the nails, I hear the cries.
He did not keep Himself away,
He was no stranger to my pain;
He walked a mile in my shoes,
He walked a mile.

Feet so dusty, cracked with heat,
But carried on by love's heartbeat.
A man of sorrows filled with grief;
Forgiveness was His anthem.
No feeble blow from tongue or pen
Could ever sway my love for Him.
Across the echoed hills He trod,
And reached into my world.

Refrain Twice

Woh, woh, woh, woh.
He walked a mile.
He walked a mile.
Woh, woh, woh, woh.
Woh, woh, woh, woh.

Heal Me

Words and Music by Kevin Stokes and Connie Harrington

recorded by Aaron•Jeoffrey

It's another good-to-see-you Sunday morning.
Oh, I hardly hear the words roll off my tongue.
Looking in myself for signs of something that's long gone.
Oh, I stumble through a verse that says You love me.
As the voices echo, my thoughts drift away.
And I close my eyes, ashamed I'm feeling nothing.
And I pray, I pray:

Refrain:
Heal me,
Heal these eyes, heal this heart, heal my mind.
Breathe Your breath of life.
Heal me,
Wake my soul from this sleep.
Give me back the joy of when I first believed.
Heal me.

Oh, I lose myself to one more day's indifference,
When my eyes are ev'rywhere but fixed on You.
I don't have the strength to overcome this distance,
But You do, You do.

Refrain

Oh, heal me.

I don't wanna waste another minute
Taking all Your love for granted.
I just wanna feel Your Holy Spirit rushing over me.

Refrain

Oh, heal me.

He'll Do Whatever It Takes

Words and Music by Dan Dean

recorded by Phillips, Craig & Dean

You don't know just how far away from home I've been
She said as she looked into my eyes.
Could it be I've strayed beyond mercy's outstretched hand
And now His grace no longer stoops to hear my cry?

You see, I just want to know:
Tell me, how far will He go.
Will He still reach to me in spite of where I've been?
And I told her—

Refrain:
He'll do whatever, whatever it takes.
His grace reaches lower than your worst mistake.
And His love will run farther
Than you can run away, my friend.
He'll do whatever, whatever it takes.

He'll do whatever It takes.

I've heard His love is patient, that He always hears a prayer
And that His love will follow you despite the miles.
My best years in life I wasted, why would He even really care?
What have I to give that He would find worthwhile?

You see, I just want to know:
Tell me, how far will He go.
Will He still reach to me in spite of who I am?
Let me tell you—

Refrain

He'll do whatever—

He'll keep reaching until He finds a way
To bring you back where you belong.
Come on back home.

Refrain

He'll do whatever it takes.
Whatever it takes.
He'll do whatever it takes.

Heaven and Earth

Words and Music by John Hartley and Chris Eaton

recorded by Nichole Nordeman

You are the one, Ruler of heaven and earth.
Given a name high above all other names.
And all things made were made by You.
I'm so amazed I belong to You.

Refrain:
How can one, one so holy be prepared
To live inside of a heart like mine?
I'll never know why,

But as I,
I go deeper I know.
I can be certain that love is a gift
Wrapped up in the mystery of You.

You came down, lived as the least of all men.
You suffered and died, bearing unbearable shame.
Now here in the shadow of Your cross,
You wash me clean of all I'm guilty of, of all I'm guilty of.

Refrain

But as I, I go deeper into life.
I can be certain that love is a gift
Wrapped up in the mystery of You.

Refrain

But should I leave You out day by day?

Lord, remind me that love is a gift
Wrapped up in the mystery of You.
Oh, yes, it is.
Hey, yeah, love is a gift
Wrapped up in the mystery of You.

Heaven in the Real World

Words and Music by Steven Curtis Chapman

recorded by Steven Curtis Chapman

I saw it again today,
In the face of a little child
Lookin' through eyes of fear and uncertainty.
It echoed in a cry for freedom
Across the street and across the miles,
Cries from the heart to find the missing part.

Where is the hope,
Where is the peace,
That will make this life complete
For ev'ry man, woman, boy, and girl
Lookin' for heaven in the real world.

To stand in the pourin' rain
And believe the sun will shine again,
To know that the grave is not the end,
To feel the embrace of grace
And cross the line where real life begins
And know in your heart you've found the
    missing part.
There is a hope,
There is a peace
That will make this life complete
For ev'ry man, woman, boy, and girl
Lookin' for heaven in the real world.
Heaven in the real world.

It happened one night with a tiny
    baby's birth,
And God heard creation cryin',
And He sent heaven to earth.
He is the hope, He is the peace
That will make this life complete
For ev'ry man, woman, boy, and girl
Lookin' for heaven in the real world.

He is the peace
That will make this life complete
For ev'ry man, woman, boy, and girl
Lookin' for heaven in the real world.

Heaven has come to the real world.
Heaven has come to the real world.

Repeat and Fade:
He is the hope, He is the peace.
Jesus is heaven,
Heaven in the real world.

Heaven Is Counting on You

Words and Music by Ray Boltz and Steve Millikan

recorded by Ray Boltz

Refrain:
Heaven is counting on you,
Run with a heart that is true.
Carry the cross, reaching the lost.
Heaven is counting on you.

We are standing at the end of time,
We are part of a grand design.
We are grateful to a risen Lord
For the others who've gone on before.

I hear voices in the heavenlies,
They are calling to you and me
Saying, "Rise up; There's a world to win!"
I hear them saying again,

Refrain

Many suffered, even gave their lives
For the message of the risen Christ.
Now they're watching, seated high above,
Shouting to us as we run.

Refrain

Heaven is counting on you.

There is a race, there is a prize,
There is a price to pay.
And the saints beyond cheer us on today.

Refrain Twice

His Eyes

Words and Music by Steven Curtis Chapman and James Isaac Elliott

recorded by Steven Curtis Chapman

Sometimes His eyes were gentle and filled
　with laughter,
And sometimes they cried.
Sometimes there was a fire of holy anger
In Jesus' eyes.

But the eyes that saw hope in the hopeless,
That saw through the fault to the need,
Are the same eyes that look down from
　heaven into the deepest
Part of you and me.

And His eyes are always upon us.
His eyes never close in sleep,
And no matter where you go,
You will always be in His eyes,
In His eyes.

Sometimes His voice comes calling like the
　roll of thunder,
Or the driving rain.
And sometimes His voice is quiet and we
　start to wonder
If he knows our pain.

But He who spoke peace to the water,
Cares more for our hearts than the waves,
And the voice that once said, "You're
　forgiven,"
Still says, "You're forgiven" today, today!

Sometimes I look above me when stars are
　shining,
And I feel so small.
How could the God of heaven and all cre-
　ation
Know I'm here at all?

But then in the silence he whispers,
"My child, I created you, too,
And you're my most precious creation,
I even gave my Son for you."

And His eyes are always upon you.
His eyes never close in sleep,
And no matter where you go,
You will always be in His eyes.
You will always be in His eyes.

Sometimes His eyes are gentle, and filled
　with laughter.

His Love Is Strong

Words and Music by Regie Hamm and Joel Lindsey

recorded by Clay Crosse

So many mountains that we try to climb,
So many places where we fall behind.
Deep in the struggle just to find our way
We lose the heart, we lose the faith.
Sometimes this life can tear your world apart
But you've got to remember—

Refrain:
His love is strong enough to win the fight,
His love is strong and good and right.
When the hearts gets weak and the road gets long,
His love is strong,

His love is strong.

Within the wonder of a baby's cry,
And in the thunder of the midnight sky,
Is something stronger than the heart of steel,
It's a power you can touch and feel.
So when you think that all your hope is gone,
Well, you've got to remember—

Refrain

His love is strong.

You may be walking through the darkest night
On a road that's rough,
But keep believing in the morning light
And His love will be enough.

Refrain Twice

His love is strong.

His Strength Is Perfect

Words and Music by Steven Curtis Chapman and Jerry Salley

recorded by Steven Curtis Chapman

I can do all things through Christ who gives me strength,
But sometimes I wonder what he can do through me.
No great success to show, no glory on my own
Yet in my weakness He is there to let me know:

Refrain:
His strength is perfect when our strength is gone.
He'll carry us when we can't carry on.
Raised in His power, the weak become strong.
His strength is perfect,

His strength is perfect.

We can only know the power that He holds
When we truly see how deep our weakness goes.
His strength in us begins where ours comes to an end.
He hears our humble cry and proves again:

Refrain Twice

His strength is perfect, raised in His power
The weak become strong.
His strength is perfect.
His strength is perfect.

Hold Me Jesus

Words and Music by Rich Mullins

recorded by Rich Mullins, Rebecca St. James

Verse 1:
Sometimes my life just don't make sense
   at all,
And the mountains look so big
And my faith just seems so small.

Verse 2:
And I wake up in the night and feel the dark.
It's so hot inside my soul;
There must be blisters on my heart.

Refrain:
Hold me, Jesus;
I'm shaking like a leaf.
You have been King of my glory;
Won't You be my Prince of Peace?
Hold me, Jesus,
'Cause I'm shaking like a leaf
You have been King of my glory.
Won't You be my Prince of Peace?

Repeat Verses 1 and 2

Refrain

Surrender don't come nat'rally to me.
I'd rather fight You for something I don't
   really want
Than take what You give that I need.

Surrender don't come nat'rally to me,
And I've beat my head against so many walls.
Now I'm falling down, falling on my knees.
Saying, hold me, Jesus.
Please hold me, Jesus.

Refrain Twice

My Prince of Peace?
My Prince of Peace?
My Prince of Peace?

Repeat and Fade:
Hold me, Jesus.

Hollow Eyes

Words and Music by Bob Hartman

recorded by Petra

Another day in Nigeria,
The children beg for bread.
The crops have failed, the well ran dry
When they lost the watershed.
A baby dies, its mother cries,
The children gather 'round.
They're wondering what the day will bring,
Will they be the next one found?

Do you dare to gaze into their hollow eyes,
Hollow eyes?
Are they staring holes in you with their
hollow eyes,
Hollow eyes,
Hollow eyes?

In the crowded sheds the children lay their
heads
To escape the Haitian heat.
The hunger pains drive them to the street,
Wond'ring if today they'll eat.
Some find food in the refuse heap,
Others find disease.
Some find it harder just to live
When they can die with ease.

Refrain:
Do you dare to gaze into His hollow eyes,
Hollow eyes?
Is He staring back at you with His
hollow eyes,
Hollow eyes,
Hollow eyes?

The least of these is hungry.
The least of these is sick.
The least of these needs clothing.
The least of these needs drink.
The least of these knows sorrow.
The least of these know grief.
The least of these has suffered pain,
And Jesus is His name.

Refrain

Hollow eyes, hollow eyes.

Hosanna

Words and Music by Michael W. Smith and Deborah D. Smith

recorded by Michael W. Smith

Refrain:
Blessed is He who comes in the name of the Lord!
(Hosanna, hosanna, hosanna!)
Blessed is He who comes in the name of the Lord!
(Hosanna, hosanna, hosanna!)

Verse 1:
King of Israel, welcome to our hearts,
Here to reign in righteousness.
O Ruler of the world, ruler of our hearts,
Now ascend Your throne:
You are the King of Kings, Hosanna!

Refrain

To Jerusalem, to the sons of man,
Riding in on gentle strength.
Oh, come to save Your own, come to give Your life,
The Kingdom is at hand.
You are the King of Kings, Hosanna!

Hosanna, hosanna, hosanna!
Hosanna, hosanna, hosanna!

Refrain

Repeat Verse 1

Refrain

Hosanna, hosanna, hosanna!
Hosanna, hosanna, hosanna!

House That Mercy Built

Words and Music by Matt Huesmann and Grant Cunningham

recorded by Point of Grace

The light in the distance welcomes those
Wayfaring souls come this far.
A heart grows tired, faith grows cold
Wand'ring down the winding road.
Just simply knock; the door will open.

There is a house that mercy built.
There is a place where brokenness is healed.
There is a voice saying, "Peace, be still."
There is a house that mercy built.
There is a house that mercy built.

Mercy will find you though you've given up
In the middle of what seems like nowhere.
He'll shelter you beneath his wings.
His love will cover ev'ry need.
Just simply seek and you will find.

There is a house that mercy built.
There is a place where emptiness is filled.
There is a voice saying, "Peace, be still."
There is a house that mercy built.
Rest in the house that mercy built

With blood and tears.
We've nothing left to fear.
We live in grace here in the safe embrace of God.

There is a house that mercy built.
There is a place where grace has been revealed.
There is a voice saying, "Peace, be still."
There is a house that mercy built.
Rest in the hope, rest in the peace,
For there is a house that mercy built.

Household of Faith

Words by Brent Lamb
Music by John Rosasco

recorded by Steve Green

Here we are at the start
Committing to each other by His Word and from our hearts.
We will be a family in a house that will be a home,
And with faith we'll build it strong.

Refrain:
We'll build a household of faith
That together we can make,
And when the strong winds blow it won't fall down.
As one in Him we'll grow
And the whole world will know
We are a household of faith.

Now, to be a family
We've got to love each other at any cost unselfishly.
And our home must be a place that fully abounds with grace,
A reflection of His face.

Refrain

How Beautiful

Words and Music by Twila Paris

recorded by Twila Paris

How beautiful the hands that served
The wine and the bread and the sons of the earth.
How beautiful the feet that walked
The long dusty roads and the hill to the cross.

Refrain:
How beautiful,
How beautiful,
How beautiful is the body of Christ.

How beautiful the heart that bled,
That took all my sin and bore it instead.
How beautiful the tender eyes
That choose to forgive and never despise.

Refrain

And as He laid down His life,
We offer this sacrifice:
That we will live just as He died,
Willing to pay the price,
Willing to pay the price.

How beautiful the radiant Bride
Who waits for her Groom with His light in her eyes.
How beautiful when humble hearts give
The fruit of pure lives so that others may live.

Refrain

How beautiful the feet that bring
The sound of good news and the love of the King.
How beautiful the hands that served
The wine and the bread and the sons of the earth.

Refrain

How Could I Ask for More

Words and Music by Cindy Morgan

recorded by Cindy Morgan

There's nothin' like the warmth of a summer afternoon;
Wakin' to the sunlight; bein' cradled by the moon;
Catchin' fireflies at night; buildin' castles in the sand;
Kissin' mama's face goodnight and holdin' daddy's hand.

Thank You, Lord.
How could I ask for more?

Runnin' barefoot through the grass, a little hide and go seek;
And bein' so in love that you can hardly eat;
And dancin' in the dark when there's no one else around;
Bein' bundled 'neath the covers, watchin' snow fall to the ground.

Thank You, Lord.
How could I ask for more?

So many things I've thought would bring me happiness.
Some dreams that are realities today.
Such an irony: the things that mean the most to me
Are the mem'ries that I made along the way.

So, if there's anything I've learned from this journey I am on,
Simple truths will keep you goin', simple love will keep you strong.
'Cause there are questions without answers and flames that never die,
And heartaches we go through are often blessings in disguise.

So, thank You, Lord,
Ah, thank You, Lord, yeah.
How could I ask for more?

How Could You Say No

Words and Music by Mickey Cates

recorded by Julie Miller

Thorns on His head, spear in His side,
Yet it was a heartache that made Him cry.
He gave His life so you would understand.
Is there any way you could say no to this Man?

If Christ Himself was standing here,
Face full of glory and eyes full of tears,
And He held out His arms and His nail-pierced hands,
Is there any way you could say no to this Man?

Refrain:
How could you look in His tear-stained eyes,
Knowing it's you he's thinking of?
Could you tell Him you're not ready to give Him your life?
Could you say you don't think you need His love?

Jesus is here with His arms opened wide.
You could see Him with your heart,
If you'll stop looking with your eyes.
He's left it up to you, He's done all He can.
Is there any way you could say no to this Man?

Refrain

Thorns on His head, your life in His hands,
Is there any way you could say no to this Man?
Is there any way you could say no to this Man?

How Excellent Is Thy Name

Words and Music by Dick Tunney, Melodie Tunney and Paul Smith

recorded by Larnelle Harris

How excellent is Thy name, O Lord,
How excellent is Thy name!
Heaven and earth together proclaim
How excellent is Thy name!

Repeat to End

How Majestic Is Your Name

Words and Music by Michael W. Smith

recorded by Sandi Patty

Refrain:
O Lord, our Lord,
How majestic is Your name in all the earth.
O Lord, our Lord,
How majestic is Your name in all the earth.

Verse:
O Lord, we praise Your name.
O Lord, we magnify Your name,
Prince of Peace, mighty God,
O Lord God Almighty.

Refrain

Repeat Verse

Prince of Peace, mighty God,
O Lord God Almighty.

Hunger and Thirst

Words and Music by Phil Madeira

recorded by Susan Ashton

You are my shepherd; I'm Your little lamb.
You lead me by the still water here in the pastureland.
Sometimes I willfully wander;
That's when I stumble and fall.
Oh—

Refrain:
I hunger and thirst for mercy;
I hunger and thirst for Your name.
If I hunger and thirst for anything but You,
I hunger and thirst in vain.

You are my Father; I'm Your little child.
You make a place at Your table and ask me to stay awhile.
I want to stay in Your presence; I want to feast in Your hall.
Yeah—

Refrain

Heavenly Father, watch over me.
Take me where healing waters run deep.

Refrain

I hunger and thirst for Your name.
If I hunger and thirst for anything but You,
I hunger and thirst in vain.

I Am Sure

Words and Music by Michael W. Smith and Mike Hudson

recorded by Michael W. Smith

Looking at the future, who can tell you what is going on;
It seems we have become the generation of wars and bombs.
And the heart grows weak and the fear grows strong
That the day may come and it may not be very long;
And you want to run but you don't know where.
So where do you go?
I know!

Refrain:
And I tell you I am sure there will be a day,
But it will not be like the nations say.
The Lord will come when this life is through,
And His deep desire is to be with you.
Hearts will fly when the new world starts
And joy will rise like the Morning Star.
God will meet ev'ry cry of the heart,
And it's my prayer I want you to be there.

I like to think about the new creation, things that God will do;
So ev'ry now and then I stop and close my eyes:
I enjoy the view!
And the heart grows strong and the fear grows weak,
And I cannot wait for the new world to come to me;
And while I dream, oh, I pray for you
'Cause He wants you to go,
I know!

Refrain Twice and Fade

I Believe

Words and Music by Alisa Girard

recorded by Wes King

I used to close my eyes and pray the time would pass me by
So I could fly away in my dreams to anywhere unreal,
And I'd hide away from everything.
I didn't know what was real; I didn't know the truth.
There was a day when somebody introduced me to You,
And You breathed Your life in me.

Refrain:
Now I'll shout it from the mountain
That I'm not the same that I used to be.
I believe in God, believe in God.
I'm not ashamed to talk about it
To a world that slowly slips away,
That I believe in God, believe in God.

Now at the end of day when nothing seems to go my way
I've got a friend, I've got a love that's never gonna let me go.
Since You gave Your life to me.

Refrain

Oh, when I feel so alone,
He comes to sweetly say, "It's all gonna be okay."
Oh, when my emotions flow,
He comes to sweetly say, "It's all gonna be okay."

Now I'll shout it from the mountain.
Now I'll shout it from the mountain.

Refrain Twice

I Call Him Love

Words and Music by Kevin Stokes, Ty Lacy and Joanna Carlson

recorded by Kathy Troccoli

Some called Him a prophet,
Some called Him a saint,
Some couldn't believe their eyes
Or the words He had to say.
Some called Him crazy,
Some thought He was strange,
But I have felt His touch
And I'll never be the same.

Refrain:
I call Him love, I call Him mercy.
I called Him out of my darkness and pain
And He answered my need.
I call Him love, I call Him healing.
He is the One who has filled me with hope
And restored life to me.
I call Him love.

Some call Him a myst'ry,
A power without a face.
Some feel He's a distant Father
That they could not erase.
But I have felt His touch
And I'll never be the same.

Refrain

'Cause He reached out to me.
I'm overwhelmed by the grace I have received.

Refrain Twice

CONTEMPORARY CHRISTIAN

I Pledge Allegiance to the Lamb

Words and Music by Ray Boltz

recorded by Ray Boltz

I have heard how Christians long ago
Were brought before a tyrant's throne.
They were told that he would spare their lives
If they would renounce the name of Christ.
But one by one they chose to die;
The Son of God they would not deny.
Like a great angelic choir sings,
I can almost hear their voices ring.

Refrain:
I pledge allegiance to the Lamb,
With all my strength, with all I am.
I will seek to honor His commands.
I pledge allegiance to the Lamb.

Now the years have come and the years have gone
And the cause of Jesus still goes on.
Now our time has come to count the cost,
To reject this world, to embrace the cross.
And one by one let us live our lives
For the One who died to give us life.
Till the trumpet sounds on the final day,
Let us proudly stand and boldly say:

Refrain

To the Lamb of God who bore my pain,
Who took my place, who wore my shame.

I will seek to honor His commands.
I pledge allegiance to the Lamb.
I pledge allegiance to the Lamb,
With all my strength, with all I am.

I Surrender All

Words and Music by David Moffitt and Regie Hamm

recorded by Clay Crosse

I have wrestled in the darkness of this lonely pilgrim land,
Raising strong and mighty fortresses that I alone command.
But these castles I've constructed by the strength of my own hand
Are just temporary kingdoms on foundations made of sand.
In the middle of the battle I believe I've fin'lly found
I'll never know the thrill of vict'ry till I'm willin' to lay down
All my weapons of defense and earthly strategies of war.
So, I'm layin' down my arms and runnin' helplessly to Yours.

Refrain:
I surrender all my silent hopes and dreams,
Though the price to follow costs me ev'rything.
I surrender all my human soul desires
If sacrifice requires that all my kingdoms fall.
I surrender all.

If the source of my ambition is the treasure I obtain,
If I measure my successes on a scale of earthly gain,
If the focus of my vision is the status I attain,
My accomplishments are worthless and my efforts are in vain.
So, I lay aside these trophies to pursue a higher crown.
And should You choose somehow to use the life I willingly laid down,
I surrender all the triumph for it's only by Your grace
I relinquish all the glory and I surrender all the praise.

Refrain

Ev'rything I am, all I've done and all I've known
Now belongs to You.
The life I live is not my own.
Just as Abraham laid Isaac on the sacrificial fire,
If all I have is all that You desire,

Refrain

I Think I See Gold

Words by Ray Boltz
Music by Steve Millikan and Ray Boltz

recorded by Ray Boltz

I see you struggling ev'ry day.
You think, "How long can I go on this way?"
On and on, again and again,
Oh, when will this end?
You think, "I just can't go on much longer."
But inside, my friend, your faith is growing stronger.
You feel the fire burning deep in your soul.
But I want you to know,

Refrain:
I think I see gold,
I think I see gold in the fire.
Right there in the ashes is all you've desired.
Oh, it's hard as you press t'ward the goal.
Don't give up,

Don't give in, don't stop now;
I think I see gold.

Until this moment you've always believed
When life grew darkest, by faith you could see.
Open your eyes, look for the light.
You see you were right.
These lonely hours, like a fire refining
Something that's precious, something that's shining.
There in the darkness, surrounded by coals,
Is starting to glow.

Refrain

Don't stop now.

Oh, I know that He'll bring you through this somehow.
Don't give up, don't give in, don't stop now;
I think I see gold.

(Spoken:) I think I see gold.

I Will Be Free

Words and Music by Cindy Morgan

recorded by Cindy Morgan

The mountains are steep and the valleys low.
Already I'm weary, but I have so far to go.
Oh, and sorrow holds my hand and suff'ring sings me songs.
But when I close my eyes, I know to whom I belong,
Who makes me strong—

Refrain:
I will be free.
I will be free to run the mountains.
I will be free,
Free to drink from the living fountain.
Oh, I'll never turn back, 'cause He awaits

For me.
Oh, I will be free.

A wise man, a rich man in pauper's clothes.
A shepherd to lead us through the land of woes.
Though many battles I have lost, so many rivers yet to cross.
But when my eyes behold the Son who bore my loss,
Who paid the cost—

Refrain

For me.
Oh, I will be free.

Oh, oh, and I'll dance on silver moonlight,
And I'll walk through velvet fields.
Oh, and I'll run into the arms,
The arms that set me free.
Oh—

Refrain

Oh, I'll never turn back.
Don't you ever turn back 'cause someday, someday,
We're gonna see that we will be free.

I Will Be Here

Words and Music by Steven Curtis Chapman

recorded by Steven Curtis Chapman

Tomorrow mornin' if you wake up
And the sun does not appear,
I, I will be here
If in the dark we lose sight of love,
Hold my hand and have no fear
'Cause I, I will be here.

I will be here
When you feel like bein' quiet.
When you need to speak your mind,
I will listen, and I will be here.
When the laughter turns to cryin'
Through the winnin', losin' and tryin',
We'll be together,
'Cause I will be here.

Tomorrow mornin' if you wake up
And the future is unclear,
I, I will be here.
As sure as seasons are made for change,
Our lifetimes are made for years,
So I, I will be here.

I will be here,
And you can cry on my shoulder.
When the mirror tells us we're older,
I will hold you.
And I will be here
To watch you grow in beauty
And tell you all the things you are to me.
I will be here.

I will be true
To the promise I have made
To you and to the One
Who gave you to me.

I, I will be here.
And just as sure
As seasons are made for change,
Our lifetimes are made for years.

So I,
I will be here.
We'll be together.
I will be here.

I Will Be the One

Words and Music by Babbie Mason

recorded by Babbie Mason

Who will be the first to lead the way?
I will be the one.
Who will stand in the gap?
Who will watch and pray?
I will be the one.

Who will walk his brother in unity?
Who will live in faith and integrity?
Who will say to the Lord, "Here am I; send
me"?

Refrain:
I will be the one.
I will be the one that God is looking for;
I will never be ashamed.
In the name of the Lord

I'll stand and proclaim, yes, I will be the
one.
Yes, I will be the one.

Like a city on a hill, who will shine the light?
I will be the one.
In a world of darkness, who will hold it
high?
I will be the one.

Who will pray for revival all over the land?
Who will seek God's forgiveness for all our
sin?
Who will ask the Lord to touch with His
mighty hand?

Refrain

I'll stand and proclaim, yes, I will be the
one.
Yes, I will be the one.

Who will call our nation to holiness?
I will be the one.
Who will raise up a standard of righteous-
ness?
I will be the one.

Who will trust in the Lord for the rest of their
days?
Who will honor the Lord in each and every
way?
Who will give God the glory and all of the
praise?

Refrain

I'll always proclaim, yes, I will be the one.
Yes, I will be the one.

I will be the one.
I will be, I will be the one.
I will be, I will be the one.

I'll Be Believing

Words and Music by Geoffrey P. Thurman and Becky Thurman

recorded by Point of Grace

When I'm walking the straight and narrow,
Sometimes life throws a little curve.
If I slip on the stones beneath me,
Will I lose my nerve?
Looking up when I've hit the bottom,
Giving thanks that the motion's stopped
I still have a rock to hold to
If the bottom drops.
Out—

Refrain:
Here on my own I won't be alone.
I'll keep believing you.
I'll be believing.
I will be believing.
Oh, I'll be believing you.
I'll be believing, I will be believing.
Oh, I'll be believing you.

If I find all my hopes are hollow
Even if all my wells run dry?
If I'm left here with next to nothing
And I don't know why.
I'm—

Refrain Twice

Repeat and Fade:
I'll be believing, I will be believing.
Oh, I'll be believing you.

I'll Lead You Home

Words and Music by Michael W. Smith and Wayne Kirkpatrick

recorded by Michael W. Smith

Wandering the road of desp'rate life,
Aimlessly beneath a barren sky.
Leave it to Me, I'll lead you home.
So afraid that you will not be found,
It won't be long before your sun goes down.
Just leave it to Me, I'll lead you home.

Refrain 1:
Hear Me calling,
Hear Me calling.
Leave it to Me, I'll lead you home.

A troubled mind and doubter's heart,
You wonder how you ever got this far.
Leave it to Me, I'll lead you home.

Vultures of darkness ate the crumbs you left,
You've got no way to retrace your steps.

Just leave it to Me, I'll lead you home.

Refrain 1 Twice

Refrain 2:
So let it go and turn it over to the One who
Chose to give His life for you.
Leave it to Me, I'll lead you home.

Refrain 2

Leave it to Me, I'll lead you home.

Refrain 1 and Fade

In Christ Alone

Words and Music by Don Koch and Shawn Craig

recorded by Michael English

In Christ alone will I glory
Though I could pride myself in battles won.
For I've been blessed beyond measure,
And by His strength alone I overcome.
Oh, I could stop and count successes
Like diamonds in my hand,
But those trophies are not equal
To the grace by which I stand.
In Christ alone—

Refrain:
I place my trust
And find my glory in the power of the cross.
In ev'ry victory,
Let it be said of me:
My source of strength, my source of hope
Is Christ alone.

In Christ alone I will glory,
For only by His grace I am redeemed.
And only His tender mercy
Could reach beyond my weakness to my need.
Now I seek no greater honor
Than just to know Him more
And to count my gains but losses
To the glory of my Lord.
In Christ alone—

Refrain Twice

My source of strength, my source of hope
Is Christ alone.
Is Christ alone!

In Heaven's Eyes

Words and Music by Phill McHugh

recorded by Sandi Patty

A fervent pray'r rose up to heaven.
A fragile soul was losing ground.
Sorting through the earthly Babel,
Heaven heard the sound.
This was a life of no distinction,
No successes, only tries.
Yet gazing down on this unlovely one,
There was love in Heaven's eyes.

Refrain:
In Heaven's eyes there are no losers.
In Heaven's eyes no hopeless cause.
Only people like you with feelings like me,
Amazed by the grace we can find—

In Heaven's eyes.

The orphaned child, the wayward father,
The homeless traveler in the rain.
When life goes by and no one bothers,
Heaven feels the pain.
Looking down, God sees each heartache,
Knows each sorrow, hears each cry.
And looking up we'll see compassion's fire,
A blaze in Heaven's eyes.

Refrain Twice

In Heaven's Eyes.
In Heaven's Eyes.

In the Light

Words and Music by Charlie Peacock

recorded by DC Talk

I keep tryin' to find a life on my own,
Apart from You.
I am the king of excuses;
I've got one for ev'ry selfish thing I do.

Refrain 1:
What's goin' on inside of me?
I despise my own behavior.
This only serves to confirm my suspicions
That I'm still a man in need of a savior.

Refrain 2:
I wanna be in the light, as You are in the
    light.
I wanna shine like the stars in the heavens.
Oh, Lord, be my light and be my salvation,
'Cause all I want is to be in the light.
All I want is to be in the light.

The disease of self runs through my blood;
It's a cancer fatal to my soul.
Ev'ry attempt on my behalf has failed
To bring this sickness under control.
Tell me—

Refrain 1

Refrain 2

Honesty becomes me,
(There's nothing left to lose.)
Our secrets that did wrong me.
(Your presents are diffused.)
Threat has no position,
(His riches have no worth.)
Of Him that once did cover me,
(Has been sentenced to this earth,)
Has been sentenced to this earth.
Tell me—

Refrain 1

Refrain 2 Twice

In the light, in the light.
I want to be, I want to be in the light,
In the light.
I want to be, I want to be in the light.
There is no other place I want to be,
No other place that I can see,
A place to be that's just right for me.
It's gonna be, it's gonna be in the light.
When You are in the light,
It's where I need to be.
That's right where I need to be.

Into Jesus

Words and Music by Toby McKeehan, Michael Tait, Kevin Max and Mark Heimermann

recorded by DC Talk

I see the moon, a million stars are out
tonight.
Gentle reminders of the way you are.

A sea of glass, a raging storm has come to
pass.
You show your face in an array of ways.

Refrain 1:
My feet may venture to the ground,
But you will never let me down.
I can't hold it in.
My soul is screaming.

Refrain 2:
Hey you, I'm into Jesus.
Hey you, I'm into Jesus, oh, yeah.
Hey you, I'm into Jesus.
Hey you, I've seen the truth

I believe.

I know You're there; I feel Your love through
my despair.
You speak the words that ease away the pain.
My heart is free, my eyes are clear.
My soul is healed now that You have got a
hold on me.

Refrain 1

Refrain 2

And I believe.

(Oh, yes, I do.)
I still believe.
(Oh, I really do.)
I still believe.
(Hey you, the kid is back and I do declare
that the son is shining.)
I still believe.
(Hey you, the kid is back with a red alert
'cause it might be blinding.)
Hey you, the kid is back and I do declare
that the son is shining.
Hey you, the kid is back.
My feet may venture to the ground.

Refrain 1

Oh, and I believe.
Oh, I still believe.
Whoa, I'm into Jesus.
Nothing's gonna change my will.
I'm into Jesus.

Oh, one time, one time Jesus bled.
On the third He rose again.
Trying to get away.
Just want to face the dead.

One time, one time Jesus bled.
Third day rose again.
Yeah, I believe.

Into You

Words and Music by Jennifer Knapp

recorded by Jennifer Knapp

She's a skin-art junkie, all cute and petite.
All her fat-cat schemes, don't look around,
Don't you even blame me.
It's a real bad thing to spill your shades for a blind man to find it.
He can feel the whole earth move
And don't even mind it.

Refrain:
I wanna know You better than I do.
Relieve me from myself, bring me into You.
I wanna know You better than I do.
Oh, relieve me, lead me, bring me,
Bring me into

You.

She's a wanna-be hero, yeah, she try to be strong.
At the end of the hour you find that the tower
Ain't standing so tall.
It's a real hard thing to show your weakness.
If anyone can love you,
I know my King does.

Refrain

Your holiness, Your kingdom,
Your righteousness, my freedom.

She's an easy scare, she's a simple bluff,
She's a timid girl, she's in love.

Refrain

You.

Jesus Will Still Be There

Words and Music by Robert Sterling and John Mandeville

recorded by Point of Grace

Things change, plans fail,
You look for love on a grander scale.
Storms rise, hopes fade,
And you place your bets on another day.

When the goin' gets tough, when the ride's too rough,
When you're just not sure enough,

Refrain:
Jesus will still be there.
His love will never change, sure as a steady rain.
Jesus will still be there.
When no one else is true, He'll still be loving you.
When it looks like you've lost it all and you haven't got a prayer,
Jesus will still be there.

Time flies, hearts turn
A little bit wiser from lessons learned.
But sometimes weakness wins,
And you lose your foothold once again.

When the goin' gets tough, when the ride's too rough,
When you're just not sure enough,

Refrain

Jesus Freak

Words and Music by Toby McKeehan and Mark Heimermann

recorded by DC Talk

Refrain 1:
What will people think when they hear that I'm a Jesus freak?
What will people do when they find that it's true?

Separated, I cut myself clean
From a past that comes back in my darkest dreams.
Been apprehended by a spiritual force
And the grace that replaced all the me I've divorced.
I saw a man with a tat on his big fat belly.
It wiggled around like marmalade jelly.
It took me a while to catch what it said
'Cause I had to match the rhythm of his belly with my head.
"Jesus saves" is what it raved in a typical tattoo green.
He stood on a box in the middle of the city and he claimed he had a dream.

Refrain 1

Refrain 2:
I don't really care if they label me a Jesus freak.
There ain't no disguising the truth,

There ain't no disguising the truth.
Though I ain't into hiding the truth.

Kamikaze, my death is gain.
I've been marked by my Maker a peculiar display.
The high and lofty, they see me as weak
'Cause I won't live and die for the power they seek, yeah.
There was a man from the desert with naps in his head.
The sand that he walked was also his bed.
The words that he spoke made the people assume
There wasn't too much left in the upper room.

With skins on his back and hair on his face,
They thought he was strange by the locusts he ate.
You see, the Pharisees tripped when they heard him speak
Until the king took the head of this Jesus freak.

Refrains 1 and 2 Twice

No, I ain't into hiding.

People say I'm strange, does it make me stranger
That my best friend was born in a manger?
People say I'm strange, does it make me stranger
That my best friend was born in a manger?

Refrains 1 and 2 Twice

What will people think?
(What will people think?)
What will people do?
(What will people do?)
I don't really care.
(What else can I say?)
There ain't no disguising the truth.
(Jesus is the way.)

Joy in the Journey

Words and Music by Michael Card

recorded by Michael Card

Refrain:
There is a joy in the journey,
There's a light we can love on the way.
There is a wonder and wildness to life,
And freedom for those who obey.

And for all those who
Seek it shall find it,
A pardon for all who believe.
Hope for the hopeless and sight for the blind.

To all who've been born of the Spirit
And who share incarnation with Him;
Who belong to eternity, stranded in time,
And weary of struggling with sin.

Forget not the hope that's before you,
And never stop counting the cost.
Remember the hopelessness
When you were lost?

Refrain

And freedom for those who obey.

The Joy of the Lord

Words and Music by Twila Paris

recorded by Twila Paris

The joy of the Lord will be my strength.
I will not falter, I will not faint.
He is my Shepherd, I am not afraid,
The joy of the Lord is my strength.

Refrain:
The joy of the Lord,
The joy of the Lord,
The joy of the Lord is my strength.

The joy of the Lord will be my strength.
He will uphold me all of my days.
I am surrounded by mercy and grace.
The joy of the Lord is my strength.

Refrain Twice

The joy of the Lord will be my strength.
I will not waiver, walking by faith.
He will be strong to deliver me safe.
The joy of the Lord is my strength.

Refrain Four Times

Jubilee

Words and Music by Michael Card

recorded by Michael Card

The Lord provided for a time for the slaves to be set free,
For the debts to all be cancelled so His chosen ones could see
His deep desire was for forgiveness; He longed to see their liberty.
And His yearning was embodied in the Year of Jubilee.

Refrain:
Jubilee, Jubilee.
Jesus is our Jubilee.
Debts forgiven, slaves set free!
Jesus is our Jubilee.

At the Lord's appointed time His deep desire became a man:
The heart of all true jubilation, and with joy we understand.
In His voice we hear a trumpet sound that tells us we are free!
He is the incarnation of the Year of Jubilee.

Refrain

To be so completely guilty, given over to despair;
To look in to your judge's face and see a Savior there!

Refrain Twice

Judas' Kiss

Words and Music by Bob Hartman

recorded by Petra

I wonder how it makes You feel
When the prodigal won't come home?
I wonder how it makes You feel
When he'd rather be on his own?
I wonder what it's like for You
When a lamb has gone astray?
I wonder what it's like for You
When Your children disobey?

Refrain:
It must be like another thorn stuck in Your brow.
It must be like another close friend's broken vow.
It must be like another nail right through Your wrist.
It must be just like, just like Judas' kiss.

I wonder how it makes You feel
When no one seeks Your face?
I wonder how it makes You feel
When they give up in the race?
I wonder what it's like for You
When they willingly disobey?
I wonder what it's like for You
When they willingly walk away?

Refrain Twice

Just One

Words and Music by Connie Harrington and Jim Cooper

recorded by Phillips, Craig & Dean

As we change as a man,
And the answers are a dime a dozen, points
    of view are like sand
Stretchin' out as far as they eye can see.
There's a thousand diff'rent philosophies,
But—

There's just one book, and there's just
    one name
With the power to you and the grace to save.

Refrain 1:
You can search the world for another way,
But if you're lookin' for the road to beyond,

There's just one.

There's just too much at stake
To be wasting time on imitations, promises
    and claims.
There will never be a substitute
For the blood, the Word, and the simple
    truth,
'Cause—

There's just one book, and there's just
    one name
With the power to you and the grace to save.

Refrain 1

There's just one door to open,
Where truth and hope will be waiting
There on the other side.
Just one story that's never ending
With life beginning in Jesus Christ, yeah.

Refrain 1

Refrain 2:
There's just one, just one book, and there's
    just one name
With the power to heal and the grace to save

Refrains 1 and 2 and Fade

Keep the Candle Burning

Words and Music by Jeff Borders, Gayla Borders and Lowell Alexander

recorded by Point of Grace

You think you're alone there in your silent
  storm,
But I've seen the tears you've cried,
Fallin' down and tryin' to drown
The flame of hope inside.
Let me tell you now, tell you now.

Refrain:
When you're walkin' in the dead of night,
When your soul is churnin',
When your hope seems out of sight,
Keep the candle burnin'.
All it takes is one steady heart
In a world that's turnin',
Shine a light and pierce the dark.
Keep the candle burnin'.

Keep the candle burnin'.

When you're down and you're discouraged,
When the darkness clouds your view,
You've got to gather up your courage;
You know the Lord is gonna see you
  through.
Let me tell you now, tell you now.

Refrain

One ray of light always breaks through.
Follow wherever He takes you,
Wherever he takes you.

Refrain Twice

Keep the candle burnin'.

Keep the candle burnin'.
Keep the candle burnin'.
Keep the candle burnin'.
Keep the candle burnin'.
Just one steady heart in a world that's
  turnin'.

Knockin' on Heaven's Door

Words and Music by Grant Cunningham and Matt Huesmann

recorded by Avalon

Well, in my closet
A spot is worn from hours and hours upon
my knees.
I step inside.
The quiet's like a doorway to a world of
peace.

One thing I don't worry 'bout:
I can't wear my welcome out.
I keep a—

Refrain 1:
Knock, knock, knockin' on heaven's door.
I keep talk, talk, talkin' 'cause You answer,
Lord.
Won't be stop, stop, stoppin';
So be listenin' for me.
I'm knockin', knock, knockin' on heaven's
door.

I'm not a poet.
No it's not like me to speak in flow'ry words.
I'm not a prophet
Not, at least, in these parts, that would be
unheard of.

But my heart speaks loud and clear,
And since my prayers are answered here,
I keep a—

Refrain 1

Refrain 2:
Whisper what you're feeling; shout it at the
ceiling.
Nothing's gonna fall on deaf ears.

Ask Him for His mercy, pray away your
worries.
What do you want heaven to hear?

Refrain 2

Bless the world around you, pray His peace
surrounds you.
What do you want heaven to hear?

Refrain 2

Thank Him for His favor, simply praise the
Savior,
That's what I want heaven to hear.

I keep knockin';
Can't you hear me talkin'?
Oh, I won't be stoppin'.
Hear me, Lord,
I'm knockin' on heaven's door.

Refrain 1 Twice and Fade

Know You in the Now

Words and Music by Michael Card

recorded by Michael Card

Echo of history,
The light so many strain to see,
The One we talk so much about,
But rarely ever live it out.
Would You tell me why?
Was it for this You came and died:
A once-a-week observance
When we coldly mouth Your words?

Refrain:
But I long to see Your presence in reality,
But I don't know how.
Let me know You in the now.

We should confess
We lose You in our busyness.
We've made You in our image,
So our faith's idolatry.
Oh, deliver me!
Break my heart so I can see
All the ways You dwell in us,
That You're alive in me!

Refrain Twice

Lamb of God

Words and Music by Twila Paris

recorded by Twila Paris

Your only Son, no sin to hide,
But You have sent Him from Your side
To walk upon this guilty sod
And to become the Lamb of God.

Your gift of Love they crucified,
They laughed and scorned Him as He died.
The humble King they named a fraud
And sacrificed the Lamb of God.

Refrain:
Oh Lamb of God, sweet Lamb of God.
I love the Holy Lamb of God.
Oh, wash me in His precious blood,
My Jesus Christ, the Lamb of God.

I was so lost, I should have died,
But You have brought me to Your side
To be led by Your staff and rod
And to be called the Lamb of God.

Refrain

Let There Be Praise

Words and Music by Dick Tunney and Melodie Tunney

recorded by Sandi Patty

Let there be praise,
Let there be joy in our hearts.
Sing to the Lord,
Give Him the glory;
Let there be praise,
Let there be joy in our hearts.
Forever more let His love fill the air,
And let there be praise.

Repeat Until Final Bar

Let there, oh let there be praise.

Let Us Pray

Words and Music by Steven Curtis Chapman

recorded by Steven Curtis Chapman

I hear you say your heart is aching,
You've got trouble in the making,
And you ask if I'll be praying for you, please.
And in keeping with convention,
I'll say yes, with good intentions
To pray later, making mention of your needs.

But since we have this moment here at
   heaven's door,
We should start knocking now.
What are we waiting for?

Refrain 1:
Let us pray,
Let us pray, ev'rywhere in ev'ry way.
Ev'ry moment of the day,
It is the right time.

Refrain 2:
For the Father above,
He is listening with love,
And He wants to answer us,
So let us pray.

So when we feel the spirit moving,
Prompting, prodding, and behooving,
There is not time to be losing, let us pray.
Let the Father hear us saying
What we need to be conveying.
Even while this song is playing, let us pray.

And just because we say the word "Amen,"
It doesn't mean this conversation needs
   to end.

Refrain 1

Refrain 3:
Let us pray without end,
And when we finish, start again.
Like breathing out, and breathing in,
Oh, let us pray.

Let us approach the throne of grace with
   confidence,
As our prayers draw us near to the One who
   knows our needs
Before we even call His name.

Refrains 1 and 2

Refrains 1 and 3

Oh, let us pray, yeah.
Let us pray.
Oh, let us pray, yeah.
Pray this way.

Our Father, which art in heaven, Hallowed be
   Thy name.
Thy kingdom come, Thy will be done on
   earth as it is in heaven.

Repeat Twice:
Let us pray.
Let us pray, let us pray, oh, let us pray, yeah.

Listen to Our Hearts

Words and Music by Geoff Moore and Steven Curtis Chapman

recorded by Geoff Moore with Steven Curtis Chapman

How do you explain,
How do you describe
A love that goes from East to West
And runs as deep as it is wide?

Verse 2:
You know all our hopes,
Lord, You know all our fears,
And words cannot express the love we feel,
But we long for You to hear.
So—

Refrain:
Listen to our hearts,
Hear our spirit sing
A song of praise that flows from those
You have redeemed.
We will use the words we know
To tell You what an awesome God You are;
But words are not enough to tell You
   of our love,
So listen to our heats.

If words could fall like rain
From these lips of mine
And if I had a thousand years
I would still run out of time;

So if You'll listen to my heart
Ev'ry beat will say
Thank You for the life, thank You for the
   truth,
Thank You for the way.
So—

Refrain

Verse 2

Refrain

Words are not enough to tell You of our love,
So listen to our hearts.

A Little More

Words and Music by Jennifer Knapp

recorded by Jennifer Knapp

Turn Your eyes from on this way.
I have proved to live a dastardly day.
I hid my face from the saints
And the angels who sing of Your glory.
What you had in mind,
Said-a, ooh, my weakness shines.
Shine, show me grace.

Refrain:
A little more than I can give,
Little more than I deserve,
Unearth this holiness I can't earn.
It's a little more than I can give,
Little more than I deserve.

For all the sin that lives in me,
It took a nail to set me free.
Still, what I do I don't wanna do
And so goes the story.
What You had in mind,
Said-a, when we seek we'll find.
Shine, show me grace.

Refrain

With all this motivation,
I still find a hesitation deep within my soul.
Oh, and despite all my demanding,
I still find You understanding.
Show me grace,
Show me grace I know is a-oh,

Refrain

Live Out Loud

Words and Music by Steven Curtis Chapman and Geoff Moore

recorded by Steven Curtis Chapman

Live it out.
Live it out, live it out.
Oh, oh, yeah!
Here we go.

Imagine this:
I get a phone call from Regis.
He says, "Do you want to be a millionaire?"
They put me on the show and I win with two
   lifelines to spare.
Now picture this:
I act like nothing ever happened and bury
   all the money in a coffee can.

Well, I've been given more than Regis ever
   gave away.
I was a dead man who was called to come
   out of my grave.
And I think it's time for makin' some noise.

Refrain:
Wake the neighbors;
Get the word out.
Come on, crank up the music,
Climb a mountain and shout.
This is life we've been given,
Made to be lived out,
So, la la la la live out loud.

Live out loud.

Think about this:
Try to keep a bird from singing after it's
   soared up in the sky;
Give the sun a cloudless day and tell it not to
   shine.
Now think about this:
If we really have been given the gift of a life
   that will never end,

And if we have been filled with living hope,
   we're gonna overflow,
And if God's love is burning in our hearts
   we're gonna glow.
There's just no way to keep it in.

Refrain

Live out loud.

Ev'rybody, come on,
I want to hear ev'rybody sing.
La la la, La la la la, La la la
Live out loud, loud, loud.
Ev'ry corner of creation is a living
   declaration.
Come join the song we were made to sing.

Refrain Twice

Repeat and Fade:
Wake the neighbors, get the word out.
La la la, live out loud.

Living for You

Words and Music by Shauna Bolton, Chrissy Conway, Alisa Girard, Kristin Swinford and Joe Priolo

recorded by ZOEgirl

There was a time when I'd believe in
  anything but You.

I closed my eyes and let You in,
Ready to let my life begin.
It just hit me; couldn't ignore it.
Heard Your voice calling; now I know it.

Refrain:
I wanna see Your face;
I wanna speak Your name;
I wanna tell the whole world how my life
  has changed.
I'm gonna lift my voice,
Ever to sing Your praise.
As long as I'm alive, know that I, I'm
  living for You.

Lord, here I stand before You now.
I want to give You ev'rything.

No matter what may come my way,
You give me a smile they can't take away.
Holding on to all You brought me through.
You're the strength that I'll always cling to.

Refrain

Some may question what is right
In my heart I can't deny
That once I was blind, but now I see.
You have my soul and I am Yours for
  eternity.

Oh, Lord,
I wanna see Your face,
I always wanna sing Your praise.
I wanna be the first to say,
Forever I'm living for only You.

Refrain Twice

Look What Love Has Done

Words and Music by Rob Mathes and Stephanie Lewis

recorded by Jaci Velasquez

Where once the moon was just a rock spinning in the sky,
Where once the stars were only tiny points of light,
Now the moon looks like it's heaven's shining pearl.
Now those stars, they look like windows into another world.

Refrain:
Look what love has done to me,
Look what love has done.
There's poetry in all I see.
Look what love has done
And my heart is dancing through each day;
My soul is running free.

Look what love has done to me.

Where once each breath was just a sight of aching emptiness,
Where once I hardly felt the beating in my chest,
Now each breath feels like a precious kiss of life.
Now inside me beat the wings of a thousand butterflies.

Refrain

Look what love has done to me.

And I can't tell:
Was that a violin, or did You say something?
Was that lightning striking where I stand,
Or did You just reach out and take my hand?

Refrain

Look what love has done to, oh, done to me.
Look what love has done to me.
Dancing through each day.
Oh, to me.

Lord of All

Words and Music by Carman

recorded by Carman

Refrain 1:
Lord, You are wonderful, Lord, You are glorious,
You are Lord of all.
Lord, You are wonderful, Lord, You are glorious,
You are Lord of all.

Refrain 2:
You are Lord of all, faithful and true,
Lord of all, worthy are You,
Lord of all, we lift up our voice
And let the earth rejoice
That Jesus Christ is Lord of all.

Refrain 3:
Ev'ry knee shall bow, ev'ry tongue confess:
Jesus Christ is Lord of all.
Lift up your eyes, let the church arise:
Jesus Christ is Lord of all.

Refrains 1 and 2

Refrain 3 Twice

We worship and adore You, worship and adore You.
We worship and adore You, worship and adore You.
Lord of all.

Refrain 3 Twice

Ev'ry knee shall bow.
Ev'ry tongue confess.

Lord of the Dance

Words and Music by Steven Curtis Chapman and Scotty Smith

recorded by Steven Curtis Chapman

Da da da...

On the bank of the Tennessee River, in a
small Kentucky town,
I drew my first breath one cold, November
mornin'.
And before my feet had even touched the
ground,
With the doctors and the nurses gathered
'round,
I started to dance.
Yeah, I started to dance.

A little boy full of wide-eyed wonder,
footloose and fancy free.
But it would happen as it does for ev'ry
dancer,
That I'd stumble on a truth I couldn't see,
And find a longing deep inside of me.
It said,

I am the heart, I need the heartbeat,
I am the eyes, I need the sight,
I realize that I am just a body, I need a life.
I move my feet, I go through the motions,
But who'll give purpose to chance?
I am the dancer,
I need the Lord of the dance.

The world beneath us spins in circles,
And this life makes us twist and turn and
sway.
But we were made for more than rhythm
with no reason

By the One who moves with passion and
grace.
As he dances over all that He had made.

I am the heart, He is the heartbeat,
I am the eyes, He is the sight, and I see
clearly,
I am just a body, He is the life.
I move my feet, I go through the motions,
But He gives purpose to chance,
I am the dancer,
He is the Lord of the dance,
Lord of the dance.
Lord of the dance.

And while the music of His love and mercy
plays,
I will fall down on my knees, and I will pray.

Refrain:
I am the heart, You are the heartbeat,
I am the eyes, You are the sight, and I see
clearly,
I am just a body, You are the life.
I move my feet, I go through the motions,
But You give purpose to chance.
I am the dancer,
You are the Lord of the dance,

Refrain

I am the dancer,
You are the Lord of the dance.
You are the Lord of the dance.

Da da da...

Love

Words and Music by Bob Hartman

recorded by Petra

Love is patient, love is kind;
No eyes of envy, true love is blind.
Love is humble, it knows no pride;
No selfish motive hidden inside.

Love is gentle, makes no demands;
Despite all wrong, true love still stands.
Love is holy, love is pure;
It lasts forever, it will endure.

Refrain:
Love knows when to let go.
Love knows when to say no.
Love grows in the light of the Son,
And love shows the world
That the Son of Love has come.

Love is loyal, believes the best;
It loves the truth, love stands the test.
Love is God sent in His Son;
Love forgives all we have done.

Refrain

In this world where hatred seems to grow,
True love goes against the flow
And becomes so hard to show.

In this world where push turns into shove,
We have strength to rise above
Through the power of His love.
Lord, we need to know the power of Your love.

Refrain Twice

Love Like No Other

Words and Music by Ty Lacy and John Mandeville

recorded by Point of Grace

Who would've known
This heart would stumble on someone
As great as You
Out of the blue?

Who would've guessed that I would fall so
    deep
In a hope as true as the one I found in You?
Heaven's hands lead me to faith's open door.
I'm surrounded by a grace this soul just
    can't ignore.

Refrain:
Lord, I'm livin' in a love like no other,
Lost in mercy like I've never known.
Lord, I'm trustin' in a love like no other to
    lead me on.

Who would've cared enough to reach beyond
My thin disguise to heal my life?
Who would've dared to wear the shame
I carried deep inside; to be my sacrifice,
Saving me from myself in the nick of time?
Forgiveness found its way into this heart of
    mine.

Refrain

Unconditionally You embrace all that I am.
It's beyond all reason, it's a love I'll never
    understand.

Refrain

Lord, I'm livin' in a love like no other.
Lord, I'm trustin' in a love like no other to
    lead me on.

Refrain

Lord, I'm livin' in a love like no other.
Lord, I'm trustin' in a love like no other to
    lead me on.
To lead me on, to lead me on.

Love of Another Kind

Words and Music by Richard Mullins, Wayne Kirkpatrick, Amy Grant and Gary Chapman

recorded by Amy Grant

Verse 1:
They say love is cruel, they say love is rather fragile,
But I've found in you a love of another kind.
They say love brings hurt, I say love brings healing,
Understanding first it's a love of another kind.

Refrain:
The love I know
Is a love so few discover.
They need to know
Jesus' love is like no other.

Verse 2:
They say love won't last, I say love is never ending,
'Cause in you I have a love of another kind.
They would change their tune, they would add another measure,
If they only knew this love of another kind.

Refrain

Verse 1

Verse 2

This love of another kind,
A love of another kind,
A love of another, a love of another kind.

Repeat and Fade:
Give me love.
You say love.

Love One Another

Words and Music by Michael W. Smith and Wayne Kirkpatrick

recorded by Michael W. Smith

I had a dream that I was speaking
With a prophet from the land of wise
In a crowd of people
From the land of troubled hearts.
I said, "We've come here for answers,
A solution to our world's demise."
He said the journey would be long,
But here is where you start.

Refrain
Love one another.
Love one another.
Work it in to work it out,
There could never be enough.
Love one another.
Love one another.
'Cause you know without a doubt,
You can change the world with love.

It was a simple conclusion,
But I thought that it was rather profound,
Just a fundamental law
That we should all live by.
I took it into tomorrow,
Yeah, I walked the earth
But I never found any corner
Of the world where this did not apply.

Refrain

And looking out I saw no method
To the madness there.
Like in a vision from the Isle of Patmos,
I was scared.
It was a revelation,
Love is getting rare.

The people of the land united
And in my dream we all agreed
That we should start again
And this would be our creed…

Refrain and Fade

Love Will Be Our Home

Words and Music by Steven Curtis Chapman

recorded by Sandi Patty

If home is really where the heart is,
Then home must be a place we all can share.
For even with our diff'rences,
Our hearts are much the same.
For where live is, we come together there.

Refrain 1:
Wherever there is laughter ringing,
Someone smiling, someone dreaming,
We can live together there.
Love will be our home.

Refrain 2:
Wherever there are children singing,
Where a tender heart is beating,
We can live together there
'Cause love will be our home.

With love, our hearts can be a fam'ly,
And hope can bring this fam'ly face to face.
And though we may be far apart,
Our hearts can be as one
When love brings us together in one place.

Refrain 1

Where there are words of kindness spoken,
Where a vow is never broken,
We can live together there
'Cause love will be our home.

Refrain 3:
Love will, love will be our home.
Love will, love will be our home.
Love will, love will be our home.
Love will, love will be our home.

Refrains 1, 2, and 3

Refrain 1

Lover of My Soul

Words and Music by Michael Omartian and Amy Grant

recorded by Amy Grant

When I see the winter turning into spring,
It speaks to this heart of mine more than anything.
Underneath a blanket of snow, cold and white,
Something is stirring in the still of the night.

And then the sun comes up, slowly with the dawn.
This is the kind of feeling that I hang my hope upon.
There is a love and beauty in all that I see.
And no one, nobody is explaining You to me.

Refrain:
And maybe my eyes can't see,
But You are surrounding me here in the wind and rain;
The things that I know.
Tender and sweet and strong as my need,
I know the voice,
I know the touch;
Lover of my soul.

And when the ev'ning comes, the sunlight fades to red.
And time and time again I whisper in my head,
"Give me strength, give me faith to fully believe
That the Maker of this whole wide world is a Father to me."

Refrain

Man of God

Words and Music by Audio Adrenaline

recorded by Audio Adrenaline

Sometimes I'm a liar, sometimes I'm a fake.
Sometimes I'm a hypocrite ev'rybody hates.
Sometimes I'm a poet, sometimes I'm a
preacher.
Sometimes I watch life go by, sitting on the
bleachers.
But—

Refrain 1:
I've never been left alone
In any problem that I've known
Even though I'm to blame.
There were times when things were dark
And I've been known to miss the mark
But someone fixed my aim.

Refrain 2:
Sometimes I'm a man of God.
Sometimes I'm alright.
And sometimes I lay down,
Close my eyes and pray to God.

Sometimes I don't feel good.
It's hard to start the day.
It's hard to climb the obstacles that
sometimes come my way.
If I make it, I'm a good man; am I a bad
man if I fail?
I know I'm never good enough so I let
grace prevail.
Oh—

Refrains 1 and 2

I'm ready for the night.

Right now, I'm alright.
Right now, I'm alright.
Sometimes I'm alright.
I'm alright.
I'm alright.
Thank God.
Thank God.
'Cause—

Refrain 2 Twice

I'm ready for the night.

A Man You Would Write About

Words and Music by Billy Simon

recorded by 4HIM

From the time time began
You always chose a man
To lead the people safely by Your way,
To be a voice and echo what You say;

Like David or Abraham;
Your Word is full of such men.
And if the Bible had no closing page,
And still was being written to this day,
Oh—

Refrain:
I want to be a man
That you would write about,
Oh, a thousand years from now
That they could read about;
Your servant of choice
In whom You found favor,
A man who heard Your voice.

Generations away
It's my prayer, they will look back and say,
"Oh to have that kind of faith and love,
What a solid man of God he was."
Yeah, yeah!

Refrain Twice

A man who heard Your voice.

A Maze of Grace

Words and Music by Grant Cunningham and Charlie Peacock

recorded by Avalon

I run; I fall; I walk.
I sometimes crawl.
I give; I take; I bend,
And yet somehow I break.

I get dizzy from all this spinning 'round.
I'm determined but wonder where I'm
    bound.
I've learned to follow the sweet familiar
    sound
Of Your voice.

Refrain 1:
The straight and narrow twists and turns.
I make my way, and every day I live I learn
    to follow You.
You walk me through a maze of grace.

I stand; I sway;
I reach for You.
I push away.
I'm spent; I'm saved.
I disobey, yet I behave.

In my personal struggle to break free,
The only piece for the puzzle that I need
Is just to follow the sweet familiar lead
Of Your love.

Refrain 1

Refrain 2:
I'm lost in You and there I'm found.
You're gently guiding every time I turn
    around.
It's no surprise to see my life's a maze of
    grace.

Refrains 1 and 2 Twice

The Measure of a Man

Words and Music by Stephanie Lewis, Mark Harris and Don Koch

recorded by 4HIM

This world can analyze and size you up
And throw you on the scales;
They can IQ you and run you through their
    rigorous details.
They can do their best to rate you,
And they'll place you on their charts,
And then back it up with scientific smarts.

But there's more to what you're worth
Than what their human eyes can see.
Oh—

Refrain:
I say the measure of a man
Is not how tall you stand,
How wealthy or intelligent you are.
'Cause I found out the measure of a man
God know and understands;
For He looks inside to the bottom of your
    heart.
And what's in the heart defines the measure
    of a man.
Oh, yeah, yeah.

Well, you can doubt your worth and search
For who you are and where you stand,
But God made you in His image when He
    formed you in His hands.

But He looks at you with mercy,
And he sees you with His love.
You're His child and that will always be
    enough.

For there's more to what you're worth
Than you could ever comprehend.
Oh—

Refrain

You can spend your life pursuing physical
    perfection.
There is so much more, more than ever
    meets the eye.
For God looks through the surface,
And He defines your worth by what is on the
    inside.

Refrain Twice

Yeah, what's in the heart defines,
Yeah, what's in the heart defines the measure
    of a man.
Oh, yeah, yeah.
I know, I know, I know.
Yeah, yeah, yeah, yeah, yeah.

Mercy Came Running

Words and Music by Dan Dean, Dave Clark and Don Koch

recorded by Phillips, Craig & Dean

Once there was a holy place,
Evidence of God's embrace;
And I can almost see mercy's face pressed against the veil.
Looking down with longing eyes
Mercy must have realized
That once His blood was sacrificed freedom would prevail.

And as the sky grew dark and the earth began to shake,
With justice no longer in the way,

Refrain:
Mercy came a runnin' like a pris'ner set free,
Past all my failures to the point of my need;
When the sin that I carried was all I could see
And when I could not reach mercy,
Mercy came a runnin' to me.

Once there was a broken heart,
Way too human from the start;
And all the years left it torn apart, hopeless and afraid.
Walls I never meant to build
Left this pris'ner unfulfilled.
Freedom called but even still it seemed so far away.

I was bound by the chains from the wages of my sin,
Just when I felt like givin' in,

Refrain

Sometimes I still feel so far, so far from where I really should be.
He gently calls to my heart just to remind me:

Refrain and Fade

The Message

Words and Music by Michael Omartian, Mark Harris and Don Koch

recorded by 4HIM

The fields are white and now the time has come,
For there's a harvest, there is work left to be done.
Lord, here am I, I will be the one,
I'm committed to the finish until the setting of the sun.
Lord, I will be faithful in all I say and do.

Refrain:
To live a love that never fails,
Love my neighbor as myself,
And to give 'til there is nothin' left to give.
To live a faith that never dies,
To be crucified with Christ;
Until all that lives through me is the message.

I can't ignore what's right before my eyes,
For all around this work is searchin' for a sign;
Outside the door they're livin' in the night,
And the light that lives within me is the hope they long to find.
So I must be faithful in all I say and do.

Refrain

If we all will work together
We can make this world a better place to live.
We can make a diff'rence if we try.

Refrain Twice

Repeat Six Times:
Is the message.

Mirror

Words and Music by Rebecca St. James and Tedd Tjornhom

recorded by Rebecca St. James

May the words of my mouth please You, dear God.
May the thoughts of my heart say to You
That all that I desire is to be with You forever.

Refrain 1:
Lord, I pray,
I pray that You take me,
Make me beautiful to You.
Create me so I mirror You.

Refrain 2:
Take me, make me an image of You.
Lord, I want to mirror You.

Let the words of my mouth please You, dear God.
May the thoughts of my heart be as Yours.
'Cause all that I desire is to be here with You forever.

Refrains 1 and 2

Oh, Lord, I do.
Break me out of my complacency,
Breathe Your breath of life into my soul,
Into my soul.

May the words of my mouth please You.
Take me, make me beautiful to You.
Create me so I mirror You.

Refrain 2 Twice

Repeat and Fade:
Mirror, mirror, mirror, mirror, mirror, mirror You.
I long to—

The Mission

Words and Music by Randall Dennis and Jon Mohr

recorded by Steve Green

There's a call going out across the land in ev'ry nation,
A call to all who swear allegiance to the cross of Christ;
A call to true humility, to live our lives responsibly,
To deepen our devotion to the cross at any price.

Let us then be sober, moving only in the Spirit,
As aliens and strangers in a hostile, foreign land.
The message we're proclaiming is repentance and forgiveness,
The Author of salvation to the dying race of man.

Refrain:
To love the Lord our God
Is the heartbeat of our mission,
The spring from which our service overflows.
Across the street or around the world,
The mission's still the same:
Proclaim and live the truth in Jesus' name!

As a candle is consumed by the passion of the flame,
Spilling light unsparingly throughout a darkened room,
Let us burn to know Him deeper, then our service, flaming bright,
Will radiate His passions and blaze with holy light.

Refrain Three Times

To love the Lord our God is the heartbeat of our mission.
To love the Lord our God is the heartbeat of our mission.

Mission 3:16

Words and Music by Carman

recorded by Carman

We can't contain what's inside,
Thunder and lightning can't hide;
Freed from the past, destined to win,
Taking the Gospel where it's never been.

Refrain:
We're on, we're on, we're on a mission,
And we'll go where the brave dare to fly.
We're on a mission,
And we know it's a race, do or die.
To know Him and make Him known is our creed,
Letting the fire be freed;
Mission three-sixteen.

We don't know what we will find
Deep behind enemy lines.
We are the called, we are the few,
Ready to serve Him and willing to do.

Refrain

He did not come into the world but to save us.
He came so he could set us free, not to enslave us.

Freely we received, freely we must give,
The message of salvation to live,
Yes, to live.

Refrain

Mission three-sixteen.
Mission three-sixteen.
You're on.

More to This Life

Words and Music by Steven Curtis Chapman and Phil Naish

recorded by Steven Curtis Chapman

Today I watched in silence as people passed
 me by,
And I strained to see if there was something
 hidden in their eyes,
But they all looked back at me as if to say,
"Life just goes on."

The old, familiar story told in diff'rent ways;
"Make the most of your own journey, from
 the cradle to the grave."
And dream your dreams tomorrow, because
 today
Life must go on.
Oh! But there's—

Refrain:
More to this life than livin' and dyin',
More than just tryin'
To make it through the day,
More to this life,
More than these eyes alone can see,

And there's more than this life alone can be.

Tonight he lies in the silence, starring into
 space,
And looks for ways to make tomorrow
 better than today.
But in the morning light it looks the same,
Life just goes on.

He takes care of his family, he takes care of
 his work,
And ev'ry Sunday mornin' he takes his place
 at the church.
But somehow he still feels the need to
 search,
But life still goes on.
Oh! But there's—

Refrain

And there's more than this life alone can be.

So where do we start to find ev'ry part
Of what makes this life complete?
If we turn our eyes to Jesus, we'll find
Life's true beginning is there at the cross
 where He died.
He died to bring us—

Refrain Twice

Repeat and Fade:
More to this life.

More Than You Know

Words and Music by Lisa Kimmey-Bragg, Michael Bragg and Todd Collins

recorded by Out of Eden

I know you walk around this life without hope
Just trying to figure out a way you can cope.
Well, you do so many things to escape your fears
That you will never make it.
You'll always have to fake being happy.

I know the truth; you can believe it or not.
There's a way out of this living,
But your trust you must be giving willingly.
Someone to rescue you from all your disgrace
Who will show you all His mercy, love, and grace.

More than you know, more than you could ever dream.
(It is waiting just for you.)
There's so much more waiting for you than it seems
If you'll only believe.

I know you wonder what your life's all about;
When it comes to your future you have your doubts.
There's only one who can make you feel secure,
Who will lead you through this life.
(Where you'll spend eternity, you can be sure.)

You think the only heaven you'll ever know is a little bit of the sky
You see when your troubles seem to go for a little while.
There's a more lasting pleasure, a full measure of joy and peace
When you look inside and know you've been set free.

More than you know, more than you could ever dream.
(If you give your life away today.)
There's so much more waiting for you than it seems
If you'll only believe.

You think the only heaven you'll ever know is a little bit of the sky
You see when your troubles seem to go for a little while.
There's a more lasting pleasure, a full measure of joy and peace
When you look inside and know you've been set free.

Oh, yeah.
Free, yeah.
Oh, yeah, here it is!

More than you know, more than you could ever dream.
There's so much more waiting for you than it seems
If you'll only believe.

More than you know, more than you could ever dream.
There's so much more waiting for you,
It's waiting just for you, if you'll just let it go.
If you open your eyes.
It's waiting just for you if you'll just realize.
It's waiting just for you, much more than you'll ever know.
It's waiting just for you, it's waiting just for you,
If you'll open your eyes, if you'll realize.
It's waiting for you.

My Faith Will Stay

Words and Music by Cheri Keaggy

recorded by Cheri Keaggy

My faith will stay, my faith will grow,
Sometimes fast, sometimes slow.
Through the wind and through the rain,
By Your grace my faith will stay.

The water comes, I try to float.
I feel alone without a boat,
But then I look across the sea
And find a rope reaching to me.

And in that moment there's no doubt,
When you come in, the fear goes out.
And then the truth, I fin'lly see
Through the storm, I still believe.

My faith will stay, my faith will grow,
Sometimes fast, sometimes slow.
Through the wind and through the rain,
By Your grace my faith will stay.

Looking back into the years
There is a joy and there are tears.
But in Your wisdom I have grown,
Greater strength I've never known.

My faith will stay, my faith will grow,
Sometimes fast, sometimes very slow.
Through the wind and through the rain,
By Your grace my faith will remain.

My faith will stay, my faith will grow,
Sometimes fast, sometimes very slow.
Through the wind and through the rain,
Through it all, my faith will stay.

I believe in the things that my eyes can't even
    see,
Like the wind blows through the trees.
God has moved His hand in me so gracefully.
God has moved His hand in me.

Through the wind and through the rain,
By Your grace my faith will stay.

My faith will stay, my faith will grow,
Sometimes fast, sometimes slow.
Through the wind and through the rain,
By Your grace my faith will stay.

My faith will stay, my faith will grow,
Sometimes fast, sometimes slow.
Through the wind and through the rain,
By Your grace my faith will remain.

My faith will stay, my faith will grow,
Sometimes fast, sometimes very slow.
Through the wind and through the rain,
Through it all, my faith will stay.

My Turn Now

Words and Music by Steven Curtis Chapman and Brent Lamb

recorded by Steven Curtis Chapman

Well, it's my turn now, my turn now.
Hey, my turn to give my life away.

I close the book and I shake my head,
Sometimes I can't believe the things I've
   read.
I don't deserve what he did for me.
Hey, hey—

He gave His love and His life away,
And now He's asking me to do the same,
So I'm gonna give Him all I am,
And all I ever hope to be.
'Cause it's—

Refrain:
My turn now.
Well, it's my turn now,
My turn to give my life away.

I open up the book and look again.
I read the stories of the faithful men
Who gave up all they had to follow Him.
Yeah, yeah—

He used the strong and He used the weak.
He even gave the timid words to speak.
He called whoever listened then,
And now His call goes out again.
And it's—

Refrain Twice

My turn to say, "I love Him."
My turn to let Him know
My life is His so where He leads me
That's where I will go.
'Cause it's—

Refrain Five Times and Fade

My Utmost for His Highest

Words and Music by Twila Paris

recorded by Twila Paris

When the Savior came to earth,
Answer to the endless fall,
He became a man by birth
Then He died to save us all.

May we never come to Him
With half a heart.
All that He deserves is nothing less
Than all I am and all you are.

Refrain:
For His highest, I give my utmost.
To the King of Kings, to the Lord of Hosts,
For His glory, for His goodness,
I will give my utmost for His highest.

Standing in this holy place,
Let us all remember here,
Covered only by His grace,
We are bought with blood so dear.

May we never bring a lesser offering,
He alone is worthy to receive
The life we live,
The song we sing.

Refrain

Any dream that tries
To turn my heart will be denied.
Anything at all that weighs me down
I will gladly cast aside.

Refrain

Never Gonna Be as Big as Jesus

Words and Music by Audio Adrenaline

recorded by Audio Adrenaline

I could move to Hollywood; yeah, get my
  teeth capped.
I know I could be a big star on the silver
  screen.
And just like James Dean, I could be a star.

I could climb the corp'rate ladder; buy,
  sell, and liquidate.
Maybe be just like the Beatles; melodic
  rocking heavyweights.
I could learn to sing and dance, if I only
  had a chance.
I could be a big rock star.

I could be anything I wanted to.
Hey, I could be anything, but one thing's
  true.

Refrain:
Never gonna be as big as Jesus.
Never gonna hold the world in my hands.
Never gonna be as big as Jesus.
Never gonna build a promised land.
But that, that's alright,
Okay with me.

I could build a tower to heaven and get on
  top and touch the sky.
I could write a million songs, all designed to
  glorify.
I could be about as good, good as any
  human could
But that won't get me by.

I could do anything I wanted to.
Hey, I could do anything, but one thing's
  true.

Refrain

I could do anything I wanted to.
I could be anything, but one thing's true.

Refrain

Repeat Three Times and Fade:
Never gonna be, never gonna be, never
  gonna be,
Never gonna be, never gonna be,
Never gonna be as big as Jesus, as big as
  Jesus...

My Will

Words and Music by Toby McKeehan, Michael Tait, Joey Elwood and Daniel Pitts

recorded by DC Talk

I'm setting the stage for the things I love,
And I'm now the man I once couldn't be.
And nothing on earth could now ever move me,
I now have the will and the strength a man needs.

Refrain 1:
It's my will, I'm not moving,
'Cause if it's Your will
Then nothing can shake me.
And it's my will to bow and praise You,
I now have the will to praise my God.

Complexity haunts me for I am two men,
Entrenched in a battle that I'll never win.
My discipline fails me, my knowledge, it fools me,
But You are my shelter, all the strength that I need.

Refrain 1

I'm learning to give up the rights to myself,
The bits and pieces I've gathered as wealth.
They'd never compare to the joy that You bring me,
The peace that You show me is the strength that I need.

Refrain 1

We've got to be children of peace.
Don't you know, we've got to be children of peace.
And—

Refrain 2:
It's my will,
(We've got to be children of peace)
I'm not moving,
'Cause if it's Your will
Then nothing can shake me.
And it's my will,
(We've got to be children of peace)
To bow and praise You.
I now have the will to praise my God.

Refrain 2 Twice

It's Your will, it's Your will not mine.
It's Your will, it's Your will.
It's Your will, it's Your will not mine.
It's Your will, it's Your will.

Refrain 2

And don't you know we've got to be children of peace.
Don't you know, we've got to be children of peace.

No Way, We Are Not Ashamed

Words and Music by Carman

recorded by Carman

We are the children of the King;
We're not afraid to let our voices ring.

Christ is our salvation,
He's the light that shines.
We are a chosen generation,
Redeemed, sanctified and grafted in the vine.

Refrain:
No way, we are not ashamed
Of the Gospel or His name.
Holy hands are lifted high
To the name of Jesus Christ.

Refrain

There's many voices in the wind,
But only one that frees a soul from sin.

Christ is still the answer
For the world today.
There is no other name so given
Unto fallen man that he might be saved.

Refrain Three Times

Not of This World

Words and Music by Bob Hartman

recorded by Petra

We are pilgrims in a strange land,
We are so far from our homeland.
With each passing day it seems so clear
This world will never want us here.
We're not welcome in this world of wrong,
We are foreigners who don't belong.

Refrain:
We are strangers, we are aliens,
We are not of this world.

We are envoys, we must tarry
With this message we must carry.
There's so much to do before we leave,
With so many more who may believe.
Our mission here can never fail,
And the gates of hell will not prevail.

Refrain Twice

Jesus told us men would hate us,
But we must be of good cheer,
He has overcome this world of darkness,
Soon we will depart from here.

Refrain Twice

Oh, I Want to Know You More

Words and Music by Steve Fry

recorded by Steve Green

Just the time I feel that I've been caught in the mire of self,
Just the time I feel my mind's been bought by worldly wealth,
That's when the breeze begins to blow, I know the Spirit's call,
And all my worldly wanderings just melt into His love.

Refrain:
Oh, I want to know You more,
Deep within my soul I want to know You,
Oh, I want to know You.
To feel Your heart and know Your mind.
Looking in Your eyes stirs up within me cries
That say I want to know You.

Oh, I want to know You more.

And when my daily deeds ordinarily lose life and song,
My heart begins to bleed, sensitivity to Him is gone.

I've run the race, but set my own pace and face a shattered soul.
Now the gentle arms of Jesus warm my hunger to be whole.

Refrain

Oh, I want to know You.

And I would give my final breath
To know You in Your death
And resurrection.
Oh, I want to know You more.
Oh, I want to know You,
To know You more.
Oh, I want to know You more.

Oh Lord, You're Beautiful

Words and Music by Keith Green

recorded by Keith Green

Verse 1:
Oh, Lord, You're beautiful.
Your face is all I seek,
For when Your eyes are on this child,
Your grace abounds to me.

Verse 2:
Oh, Lord, please light the fire
That once burned bright and clear.
Replace the lamp of my first love
That burns with holy fear.

Refrain:
I want to take Your Word and shine it all around,
But first, help me just to live it, Lord.
And when I'm doing well,
Help me to never seek a crown,
For my reward is giving glory to You.

Verse 1

Verse 2

Refrain

Verse 1 Twice

Only the Hands

Words and Music by Steven Curtis Chapman, Eddie Carswell and Oliver Wells

recorded by Newsong

People came from ev'rywhere,
They heard a man was there who could do miracles.
There was power in His hands, He was like no other man;
Could this really be their long awaited King?

When would He rise and take His throne?
When would He make His kingdom known?
What was He waiting for?
They just didn't know.

Refrain:
Only hands that bled can bless,
Only the eyes filled with tenderness,
Only the heart that was broken for our sin.
Only the feet that walked that hill
Could love the ones who rejected Him.
Only the One who died and is living still,
Only the hands that bled.

They had listened to His words,
But few had really heard what He was telling them.
He said that He must die, and tried to tell them why,
But most of them just could not understand.

For this was the Man who raised the dead,
These were the hands that healed and fed.
He could have stopped the nails,
But He just let them go.

Refrain

Only the life He sacrificed could save us.
Only Jesus!

Refrain

People Keep Writing Him Songs

Words and Music by Phill McHugh

recorded by Truth

He must have lived the beautiful life they
  said.
He must have really risen up from the dead.

Oh, why in the world would so many souls
Have believed it for so long?
Two thousand years of people can't all be
  wrong.
No lie or deception could be that strong.

People keep praying to Him and He keeps
  on saving them
And people keep writing Him songs.
They sing alleluias to his amazing grace.
One glad morning we will see His face.
We shall behold Him farther along.

Refrain:
They keep writing Jesus new songs.
Yeah, people keep writing Him songs.
Alleluia, Alleluia.

Out come the tributes they delight to bring,
Words and music they rejoice to sing

How one way or another He rescued them
At a point where they couldn't go on.
They're happy to join the joyous throngs
Who offer up praises where the praise
  belongs.

People keep falling and He still hears us
  calling,
So, people keep writing Him songs.
I serve a risen Savior, He is El Shaddai.
Lord, hide me in the rock till the storm pass-
  es by.
I am weak but Thou art strong.

Refrain

Alleluia, alleluia.

They sing alleluia to His amazing grace.
Oh, one good morning we will see His face.
We shall behold Him farther along.
They keep writing Jesus new songs.

Repeat and Fade:
Alleluia.

People Need the Lord

Words and Music by Phill McHugh and Greg Nelson

recorded by Steve Green

Ev'ry day they pass me by.
I can see it in their eye;
Empty people filled with care,
Headed who knows where.
On they go through private pain,
Living fear to fear.
Laughter hides the silent cries
Only Jesus hears.

Refrain:
People need the Lord.
People need the Lord.
At the end of broken dreams He's the open door.
People need the Lord.
People need the Lord.
When will we realize?

People need the Lord.

We are called to take His light
To a world where wrong seems right;
What could be too great a cost
For sharing life with one who's lost?
Through His love our hearts can feel
All the grief they bear.
They must hear the words of life
Only we can share.

Refrain

That we must give our lives
For people need the Lord.
People need the Lord.

A Place Called Grace

Words and Music by Shawn Craig and Dave Clark

recorded by Phillips, Craig & Dean

So many years I heard it told:
The story of compassion.
A prodigal son who left the fold
And found no satisfaction.
On my knees, Lord,
I cried out to You, "I'm so alone,"
But if there's room in Your house for one
	more,
I'm ready to come back home.

Refrain:
I know there is a place where arms of
	compassion
Welcome me home.
Sweet mercy falls like rain.
I know there is a place

Called grace.

So many days I've trusted grace,
Yet I have to wonder,
How many times my human strength
Has kept me from surrender.
The more I learn just to lean on the cross,
The more I see.
When I fall I will fall to the place
Where mercy reaches me, reaches me.

Refrain

Called grace.

If it seems that my courage is strong,
There's just one reason.
He's my rock when my faith is all gone.
He holds me in His arms,
Gives me strength to carry on.

Refrain

I know there's a place called grace.

Place in This World

Words by Wayne Kirkpatrick and Amy Grant
Music by Michael W. Smith

recorded by Michael W. Smith

The wind is moving, but I am standing still.
A life of pages waiting to be filled.
A heart that's hopeful, a head that's full of dreams.
But this becoming is harder than it seems.
Feels like I'm—

Refrain:
Looking for a reason,
Roaming through the night to find my place in this world.
My place in this world.
Not a lot to lean on.
I need Your light to help me find my place in this world.
My place in this world.

If there are millions, down on their knees,
Among the many can You still hear me?
Hear me asking where do I belong?
Is there a vision that I can call my own?
Show me.
I'm—

Refrain Twice

Pour My Love on You

Words and Music by Gary Sadler and Dan Dean

recorded by Phillips, Craig & Dean

I don't know how to say exactly how I feel,
And I can't begin to tell You what Your love has meant.
I'm lost for words.

Refrain 1:
Is there a way to show the passion in my heart?
Can I express how truly great I think You are?
My dearest Friend.
Lord, this is my desire, to pour my love on You.

Refrain 2:
Like oil upon Your feet,
Like wine for You to drink,
Like water from my heart, I pour my love on You.
If praise is like perfume,
I'll lavish mine on You till ev'ry drop is gone.
I'll pour my love

On You.

Refrains 1

Refrain 2 Three Times

On You.
Pour my love on You.

Refrain 2 Twice

On You.

Pray

Words and Music by Rebecca St. James, Michael Quinlan and Tedd Tjornhom

recorded by Rebecca St. James

Jesus, I am broken now.
Before You I fall.
I lay me down.
All I want is You, my all.
I cry out from the ashes, burned with sin
and shame;
I ask You, Lord, to make me whole again.

For You say if I will come and will pray to
You,
There's forgiveness when I turn from me
and pray.
For you say if I come and will pray to You,
You hear me and heal me when I pray.

And your ways are not my own,
But I long for them to be, so this is what I
pray:
One with You You'll make me.
Melt me away till only You remain.

For You say if I will come and will pray to
You,
There's forgiveness when I turn from me
and pray.
For you say if I come and will pray to You,
You hear me and heal me when I pray.

Jesus, I am broken now before You.
Take me, I am Yours,

For You say if I will come and will pray to
You,
There's forgiveness when I turn from me and
pray.
For you say if I come and will pray to You,
You hear me and heal me

For You say if I will come and will pray to
You,
There's forgiveness when I turn to You and
pray.
For you say if I come and will pray to You,
You hear me and heal me when I pray, when
I pray,
When I pray, when I pray, when I pray.

Run to You

Words and Music by Twila Paris

recorded by Twila Paris

Faster now than ever, I run to You.
Now I know you better, I run to You.
I am a little older now, You know it's true.
Maybe a little wiser, too.
I run to You.

And I can see deeper than I did before.
I do believe, never have I been so sure
That I need You ev'ry minute, ev'ry day,
That I need You more than I could ever say.

Refrain:
Ooh, I run to You.
Ooh, what else would I do?
I run to You.
Ooh, I run to You.

Even on the sad days, I run to You.
Even on the good days, too, I run to You.
Even before all else fails, You know it's true.
You are the wind in my sails, I run to You.

And I can see deeper than I did before.
I do believe, never have I been so sure
That I need You ev'ry footstep, all the way.
That I need You so much more than I can say.

Refrain Twice and Fade

Say the Name

Words and Music by Margaret Becker and Charlie Peacock

recorded by Margaret Becker

A more sweeter sounding word these lips have never said;
A gentle name so beautiful my heart cannot forget.
Just a whisper is enough to set my soul at ease.
Just thinking of this name brings my heart to peace.

Refrain:
Say the name
(Jesus)
Say the name that soothes the soul;
The name of the gentle healing and peace immutable.
I'll say the name that has heard my cry,
Has seen my tears and wiped them dry.
From now until the end of time I'll say the name.

May I never grow so strong that my heart cannot be moved.
May I never grow so weak that I fear to speak the truth.
I will say this holy name no matter who agrees,
For no other name on earth means so much to me.

Refrain

With all the honor I can find,
With all my heart, my soul, my mind
I'll say the name.
Without defense, without shame,
I will always speak the name, oh, of Jesus.

Refrain

From now until the end of time, say the name.

Scandalon

Words and Music by Michael Card

recorded by Michael Card

The seers and the prophets had foretold it long ago,
That the long awaited One would make men stumble;
But they were looking for a king to conquer and to kill.
Who'd have ever thought He'd be so meek and humble?

Refrain:
He will be the truth that will offend them one and all;
The stone that makes men stumble
And a rock that makes them fall.
Many will be broken so that He can make them whole,
And many will be crushed
And lose their own soul.

Along the path of life there lies this stubborn scandalon,
And all who come this way must be offended.
To some He is a barrier, to others He's the way;
For all should know the scandal of believing.

Refrain

It seems today the scandalon offends no one at all;
The image we present could be stepped over.
Could it be that we are like the others long ago?
Will we ever learn that all who come must stumble?

Refrain Twice

Secret Ambition

Words and Music by Michael W. Smith, Wayne Kirkpatrick and Amy Grant

recorded by Michael W. Smith

Young man upon the hillside,
Teaching new ways.
Each word winning them over;
Each heart a kindled flame.
Old men watch from the outside
Guarding their prey.
Threatened by the voice of the paragon
Leading their lambs away,
Leading them farther away.

Refrain:
Nobody knew His secret ambition;
Nobody knew His claim to fame.
He broke the old rules steeped in tradition;
He tore the Holy veil away.
Questioning those in powerful position;
Running to those who called His name.
But nobody knew His secret ambition
Was to give His life away.

His rage shaking the temple,
His word to the wise,
His hand healing on the seventh day,
His love wearing no disguise.
Some say, "Death to the radical,
He's way out of line!"
Some say, "Praise be the miracle!
God sends a blessed sign,
A blessed sign for the troubled times."

Refrain Twice

No, no, no, no.
I tell you nobody knew
Until He gave His life away.
No!

Serve the Lord

Words and Music by Carman

recorded by Carman

I believe in God the Father, Jesus Christ His
 only Son
And the blessed Holy Spirit distinct, yet
 Three in One.
I believe there is forgiveness for everything
 we've done.
That is why all the more I will serve Him.

I believe the Son of God was crucified upon
 the tree
And laid within a borrowed tomb not far
 from Calvary.
I believe He rose up from the dead, alive
 for all to see.
That is why all the more I will serve Him.

Refrain:
I have made my decision, I have staked my
 claim.
I have drawn the line in the sand and I'll
 not be ashamed.
With the world behind me and the cross
 before,
By the grace of God I will serve the Lord.

I believe you must be born again.
John three-sixteen is true.
The old life can be washed away, ev'rything
 made new.
And I believe the love of God can somehow
 find its way to you.
That is why all the more I will serve Him.
And—

Refrain

And I know when Satan and his minions
 come to torment me,
When I invoke the name of Jesus, ev'ry
 demon has to flee.
I know the time will come when Christ
 returns again someday.
Till then, there's just one name on earth
 whereby men can be saved.

I believe there is a right and wrong, a time
 to live and die.
And the Bible is the blueprint that all men
 should live by.
I believe I'm not alone with my faith in Jesus
 Christ.
That is why all the more we will serve Him.

We have made our decisions, we have staked
 our claim.
We have drawn the line in the sand and we
 won't be ashamed.
With the world behind us and the cross
 before us,
By the grace of God we will serve,
By the grace of God we will serve the Lord

Refrain

By the grace of God I will serve the Lord.
By the grace of God I will serve the Lord.

Shepherd of My Heart

Words and Music by Dick Tunney and Mark Baldwin

recorded by Sandi Patty

Maker of this heart of mine, You know me very well,
You understand my deepest part more than I know myself.
So when I face the darkness, when I need to find my way,
I'll trust in You, Shepherd of my heart.

Keeper of this heart of mine, Your patience has no end,
You've loved me back into Your arms time and time again.
So if I start to wander like a lamb that's gone astray,
I'll trust in You, Shepherd of my heart.

Refrain:
You're the beacon of my nights,
You're the sunlight of my days,
I can rest within Your arms,
I can know Your loving ways.

So let the cold winds blow,
And let the storms rage all around,
I'll trust in You, Shepherd of my heart.

Giver of this life in me, You're what I'm living for,
For all my deepest gratitude You love me even more.
So as I walk through valleys list'ning for the Master's call,
I'll trust in You, Shepherd of my heart.

Refrain

So as I walk through valleys list'ning for the Master's call,
I'll trust in You, Shepherd of my heart.
I'll trust in You, Shepherd of my heart.

Shine

Words and Music by Peter Furler and Steve Taylor

recorded by Newsboys

Dull as dirt you can't assert
The kind of light that might persuade a strict dictator to retire.
While the army teach the poor origami,
The truth is in the proof when you hear your heart starts asking,
"What's my motivation?"

And try as you may there is no way to explain
The kind of change that would make an Eskimo renounce fur;
That would make a vegetarian barbecue hamster,
Unless you can trace this about face to a certain sign.

Refrain:
Shine, make 'em wonder what you've got,
Make 'em wish that they were not
On the outside looking bored.
Shine, let it shine before all men.
Let 'em see good works and then
Let 'em glorify the Lord.

Out of the shaker and onto the plate.
It isn't karma, it sure ain't fate that would make a Deadhead sell his van.
That would make a schizophrenic turn in his crayons.
Oprah freaks and science seeks a rationale that shall
Excuse this strange behavior.

When you let it shine you will inspire the kind
Of entire turnaround that would make a bouncer take ballet.
(Even bouncers who are happy.)
But out of the glare with nowhere to turn,
You ain't gonna learn it on "What's My Line?"

Refrain Three Times

Shine on Us

Words and Music by Michael W. Smith and Debbie Smith

recorded by Phillips, Craig & Dean

Lord, let Your light,
Light of Your face shine on us.
Lord, let Your light,
Light of Your face shine on us

Refrain:
That we may be saved,
That we may have life
To find our way
In the darkest night.

Let Your light shine on us.

Lord, let Your grace,
Grace from Your hand fall on us.
Lord, let Your grace,
Grace from Your hand fall on us

Refrain

Let Your grace fall on us.

Lord, let Your love,
Love with no end come over us.
Lord, let Your love,
Love with no end come over us

Refrain

Let Your love come over us.
Let Your light shine on us.

Sing Your Praise to The Lord

Words and Music by Richard Mullins

recorded by Amy Grant; Rich Mullins

Refrain:
Sing your praise to the Lord,
Come on ev'rybody,
Stand up and sing one more hallelujah.
Give your praise to the Lord,
I can never tell you
Just how much good that it's gonna do ya.

Just to sing anew the song your heart learned to sing
When He first gave His life to you,
The life goes on and so must the song.
You gotta sing again the song born in your soul
When you first gave your heart to Him, sing His praises.
Once more

Refrain

Just to sing aloud the song that someone is dying to hear
Down in the madd'ning crowd,
As you once were before you heard the song.
You gotta let them know the truth is alive
To shine up on the way so maybe they can go sing your praises.
Once more

Refrain

Just to let the name of the Lord be praised
Both for now and evermore, praise Him, all you servants.

Refrain

Just to sing, sing, sing.
Come on, sing, sing, sing.
Let me hear ya now,
Sing, sing, sing.

Signs of Life

Words and Music by Steven Curtis Chapman

recorded by Steven Curtis Chapman

Come in, base, I've landed my ship on a planet here in space.
This is the one they say is inhabited by the human race.
And I'm going out to look around and see what's here,
And I'll tell you what I find.

Confirmation on the inhabitants, they're running ev'rywhere.
Their technology is beyond what I've seen anywhere.
But I'm trying to communicate, and they don't hear me.
Seems like for all I'm findin', I can't find the most important thing.

Where are the signs?
Where are the signs of life?
The love that proves there is a beating heart inside.
Where are the signs?
Where are the signs of life?
The compassion and concern that make this world turn.
Where are the signs of life?
Yeah, yeah, yeah, yeah, yeah.

Now, I've got crayons rolling around in the floorboard of my car,
Bicycles all over my driveway, bats and balls all over my yard,
And there's a plastic man from outer space sitting in my chair.
The signs of life are ev'rywhere.

But I've got questions rolling around in the corners of my mind,
If it's true I live in a world where hope has all but died.
And if I really have a living love alive in me,
How am I letting it be known, how am I letting it be seen?

Refrain:
These are the signs, these are the signs of life.
The love that proves there is a living faith inside.
These are the signs, these are the signs of life.
The compassion and concern that make this world turn.
These are the signs of life.

Signs of Life.
These are the signs of life.
Signs of life.
Signs of life.

Refrain

That's gonna make this world keep turnin'.

These are the signs, these are the signs of life.
A love that's flowing from the heart
Where the grace of God has left its mark.
These are the signs, these are the signs of life.
The reaching out of a servant's hand,
The giving that makes no demands,
These are the signs, these are the signs of life.
This is the loving proof of the faith inside.

Repeat and Fade:
These are the signs of life.

Sometimes He Calms the Storm

Words and Music by Kevin Stokes and Tony Wood

recorded by Scott Krippayne

All who sail the sea of faith find out before too long
How quickly blue skies can grow dark and gentle winds grow strong.
And suddenly fear is like white water pounding on the soul,
And still we sail on, knowing that our Lord is in control.

Refrain:
Sometimes He calms the storm
With a whispered, "Peace, be still."
He can settle any sea,
But it doesn't mean He will.
Sometimes He holds us close
And lets the wind and waves go wild.
Sometimes He calms the storm,
And other times He calms His child.

He has a reason for each trial that we pass through in life,
And though we're shaken, we cannot be pulled apart from Christ.
No matter how the driving rain beats down on those who hold to faith,
A heart of trust will always be a quiet, peaceful place.

Refrain

With a whispered, "Peace, be still."

Refrain

Sometimes He Comes in the Clouds

Words and Music by Steven Curtis Chapman

recorded by Steven Curtis Chapman

There are the places
I was so sure I'd find Him.
I've looked in the pages
And I've looked down on my knees.
I've lifted my eyes in expectation
To see the sun still refusing to shine.
But—

Refrain:
Sometimes He comes in the clouds.
Sometimes His face cannot be found.
Sometimes the sky is dark and gray,
But some things can only be known.
And sometimes our faith can only grow
When we can't see.

So, sometimes He comes in the clouds.

Sometimes I see me,
A sailor out on the ocean;
So brave and so sure
As long as the skies are clear.
But when the clouds start to gather,
I watch my faith turn to fear.
But—

Refrain

So, sometimes He comes in the rain.

And we question the pain
And wonder why God can seem
So far away,
But time will show us
He was right there with us.
And—

Refrain

So, sometimes He comes in the clouds.

He comes in the clouds.

Speechless

Words and Music by Steven Curtis Chapman and Geoff Moore

recorded by Steven Curtis Chapman

Words fall like drops of rain; my lips are like clouds.
I say so many things, trying to figure You out.
But as mercy opens my eyes and my words are stolen away
With this breathtaking view of Your grace.
And I am—

Refrain:
Speechless; I'm astonished and amazed.
I am silenced by Your wondrous grace.
You have saved me; You have raised me from the grave.
And I am speechless in Your presence now;
I am astounded as I consider how
You have shown us a love that leaves us speechless.

So what kind of love could this be
That would trade heaven's throne for a cross?
And to think You still celebrate over finding just one who was lost.
And to know You rejoice over us, the God of this whole universe,
It's a story that's too great for words.
And I am—

Refrain

Oh, how great is the love the Father has lavished upon us,
That we should be called the sons and the daughters of God?
Yeah, we are—

Speechless,
(We stand in awe of Your grace.)
So amazed.
(We stand in awe of Your mercy.)
You have saved us
(We stand in awe of Your love.)
From the grave.
(We are speechless.)
We are speechless.
(We stand in awe of Your cross.)
In Your presence now.
We are astounded as we consider how
(We stand in awe of Your power.)
You have shown us a love that leaves us speechless.

Repeat Twice:
We are speechless, we stand in awe of Your grace.
We stand in awe of Your mercy.
We stand in awe of Your love.
We are speechless.
We stand in awe of Your cross.
We stand in awe of Your power.
We are speechless.

Stand

Words and Music by Rebecca St. James and Regie Hamm

recorded by Susan Ashton

There is a time for healing,
There's a time for all purposes under
the sun.
There's a time for laughter.
There's a time to let go and a time to
hold on.

So we are here, but why are we waiting?
Why are we acting like dead men walking?
The time has arrived for us to arise,
Joining our hands, united together,
For this is our time to be strong.

Refrain:
This is our time to rise up,
To stand and be counted.
This is our time to believe,
To know in our God we are free.

Let the world know to Him we belong.

Lord, capture our hearts now.
Drown out the pleasures and treasures
that bind us.
Give us your courage
To be strong, to be brave and to never
back down.

There's no time to lose.
We can't be silent in a world that is dying to
find out the truth.
We've got the hope, we've got the answer.
Let's lay down our all with reckless abandon.
This is our time to be strong.

Refrain

Let the world know to Him we belong.
Now, this is our time to be strong.

Refrain

This is our time to be strong.

Refrain

There's no time to lose.
We can't be silent in a world that is dying to
find out the truth.
This is our time to be strong.

Refrain

Let the world know to Him we belong.

Steady On

Words and Music by Grant Cunningham and Matt Huesmann

recorded by Point of Grace

La da da...

Kicking up dust, heaven or bust;
We're headed for the promised land.
Since the moment we believed, we've been eager to leave,
Like a child tugging daddy's hand.

May we never forget that patience is a virtue.
Calm our anxious feet so faithful hands can serve You, Lord.

Refrain:
We run on up ahead, we lag behind You.
It's hard to wait when heaven's on our minds.
Teach our restless feet to walk beside You,
'Cause in our hearts we're already gone.

Will You walk with us, steady on?

We want to walk awhile.
We know that ev'ry mile is bringing us closer home.
We want to tell the story of sinners bound for glory,
And turn to find we're not alone.

When we walk in Your light, the lost will see you better.
As the narrow road gets crowded, Lord,
Won't You lead us steady on?

Refrain

Steady me when the road of faith gets rocky.
Oh, ready me for fears I cannot see.
Lord, won't You let me be a witness to Your promise?
Won't You steady me?
Yeah.

Refrain Twice

Will You walk with us, steady on?

Still Called Today

Words and Music by Steven Curtis Chapman

recorded by Steven Curtis Chapman

There's a hole, the size of a cruel word,
In a wounded heart somewhere that's
   learning to hide the pain.
There's a thorn stuck in the conscience of
   someone
Who spoke a word in anger, and they can't
   wash away the stain.
"Sorry's" such a hard word to say.
But while—

Refrain:
It's still called today,
Won't somebody make it right
Before the day slips into night
And the moments waste away?
While it is still called today,
Oh, we've got to say the words
That are longing to be heard;
'Cause tomorrow may be too late.
Go on and say what you need to say

While it's still called today.

There's a girl who's waiting day after day
To hear her daddy say, "I love you."
Now the days have turned to years.
There's a wall that silence has turned to
   stone
Between a man and a woman.
She's holding back the tears.
He's holding on to his fears.
And while—

Refrain

'Cause there's a time when the sun goes
   down
And the flowers are laid on the grave.
Will the tears that fall to the ground
Be the tears of regret for the words someone
   did not say?
Oh, while—

Refrain

While it's still called today.

Oh, no, no,
'Cause tomorrow may be too late.

Stubborn Love

Words and Music by Brown Bannister, Michael W. Smith, Gary Chapman, Amy Grant and Tower Sloan

recorded by Kathy Troccoli

Caught again, your faithless friend;
Don't you ever tire of hearing what a fool
  I've been?
Guess I should pray, but what can I say?
Oh, it hurts to know the hundred times I've
  caused you pain;

The "forgive me's" sound so empty when I
  never change,
Yet you stay and say "I love you still,"
Forgiving me time and time again.
It's—

Refrain:
Your stubborn love that never lets go of me;
I don't understand how you can stay;
Perfect love,
Embracing the worst in me,

How I long for your stubborn love.

Funny me, just couldn't see,
Even long before I knew you, you were
  loving me.
Sometimes I cry; you must cry too,
When you see the broken promises I've
  made to you.

I keep saying that I'll trust you, though I
  seldom do,
Yet you stay and say you love me still,
Knowing someday I'll be like you.
And—

Refrain

How I long for your stubborn love.
It's—

Refrain

And you'll never let me go,
I believe I fin'lly know,
I can't live without your stubborn love.

Take My Life

Words and Music by Cindy Morgan

recorded by Cindy Morgan

Who can say when life is over?
The silver cord breaks and our breath returns to God.
Will we walk through fields of clover
Or soar up high through valleys deep and wide?

I cannot know all that's waiting there.
But until that day, this is my prayer, oh, yes.

Refrain:
Take my life, take away all the shattered dreams in me,
And give me love that will last forever.
Take my life, give me the love that makes me free.
'Cause I believe that Your love can save
Even a wretch like me.

This race is not just for the runners.
Some of us walk while others barely crawl, hey, yeah.
We make our way through spring and winter,
Leaning on the strength that strengthens all.

And when the sunlight fades from morning
You'll still be burning in my eyes, oh, yes.

Refrain

Oh, yeah; oh, yeah.
And when the sunlight fades from morning,
Oh the morning,
You'll still be burning in my eyes, oh, yes

Refrain

Testify to Love

Words and Music by Paul Field, Henk Pool, Ralph Van Manen and Robert Riekerk

recorded by Avalon

All the colors of the rainbow, all the voices
    of the wind,
Ev'ry dream that reaches out, that reaches
    out to find where love begins,
Ev'ry word of ev'ry story, ev'ry star in ev'ry
    sky,
Ev'ry corner of creation lives to testify.

Refrain 1:
For as long as I shall live, I will testify to
    love.
I'll be a witness in the silences when words
    are not enough.
With ev'ry breath I take, I will give thanks
    to God above,
For as long as I shall live, I will testify

To love.

From the mountains to the valleys, from the
    rivers to the sea,
Ev'ry hand that reaches out, ev'ry hand that
    reaches out to offer peace,
Ev'ry simple act of mercy, ev'ry step to
    kingdom come,
All the hope in ev'ry heart will speak what
    love has done.

Refrain 1

Refrain 2:
Testify, testify...
Colors of the rainbow, voices of the wind,
Dream that reaches out where love begins,
Testify, testify...
Word of ev'ry story, star in ev'ry sky,
Corner of creation testify.

Testify, testify...
Mountains to the valleys, rivers to the sea,
Hand that reaches out to offer peace,
Testify, testify...
A simple act of mercy, kingdom come,
Ev'ry heart will speak what love has done.

Refrain 2

Refrain 1 Twice

To love.

Refrain 1

To love.

Thankful Heart

Words and Music by Bob Hartman, John Elefante and Dino Elefante

recorded by Petra

Refrain:
I have a thankful heart that You have given me.
And it can only come from You.

There is no way to begin to tell You how I feel;
There are no words to express how You've become so real.
Jesus, You've given me so much I can't repay.
I have no offering.

Refrain

There is no way to begin to tell You how I feel;
There's nothing more I can say and no way to repay
Your warming touch that melts my heart of stone.
Your steadfast love, I'll never be alone.

Refrain

I have a thankful heart; word's don't come easily.
But I am sure You can see my thankful heart.
Help me be a man of God—
A man who's after Your own heart.
Help me show my gratitude, and keep in me a thankful heart.

Refrain

Repeat and Fade:
Thankful heart.

There Is a Redeemer

Words and Music by Melody Green

recorded by Keith Green

Verse 1:
There is a redeemer,
Jesus, God's own Son.
Precious Lamb of God, Messiah,
Holy One.

Jesus, my redeemer,
Name above all names.
Precious Lamb of God, Messiah,
Oh for sinners slain.

Refrain:
Thank You, oh my Father,
For giving us Your Son,
And leaving Your spirit
Till the work on earth is done.

When I stand in glory,
I will see His face,
And there I'll serve my King forever
In that holy place.

Refrain

Repeat Verse 1

Refrain

And leaving Your spirit till the work on earth is done.

This I Know

Words and Music by Margaret Becker

recorded by Margaret Becker

Oh, Lord, won't You hold my hand
And help me to find a new place to stand?
All these changes that I've been through
Have left me with only one absolute.

This I know, only this I know
That Your love never changes as I go.
Only this I know, only this I know
That Your love never changes as I go.

Oh, Lord, I've crossed mercy lines
For what seems to be at least a thousand times.
Instead it's Your love that I see
Long, high, wide, and deep a-reachin' out to catch me.

This I know, only this I know
(Love never changes)
Never changes, never changes, no, not ever.
This I know, only this I know
That Your love never changes as I go.

It was love that first drew me, it is love that will keep me here.
Now I see love burning brightly when ev'rything else isn't clear.

This I know, only this I know
That Your love never changes as I go.
Only this I know, only this I know
That Your love never changes as I go.

Repeat and Fade:
This I know, only this I know
That Your love never changes as I go.
Only this I know, only this I know
That Your love never changes as I go.

This Is the Life

Words and Music by Shawn Craig and Leonard Ahlstrom

recorded by Phillips, Craig & Dean

This life is the life that I've chosen.
Yeah, nobody made me do it.
Feels right, givin' all my devotion.
Oh, yeah.

Take it from a man who's had a taste of both
    sides:
There's no sweeter freedom than a godly life.
I just wanna testify.
(Go ahead and testify.)

Refrain:
This is the life.
I'm where I wanna be:
Livin' from the center of a heart that's free.
Oh, I'm feelin' alright, day or night, rain or
    shine.

This is the life.
This is the life, y'all.

You think it's a dull life that I'm livin',
Yeah, you say it's such a pity:
So weak, to need a crutch of religion.
Oh, no.

Pardon me a minute but I think I need to
    say.
I don't need your sympathy so don't be
    talkin' that way.
You will see the light someday.
(You will see the light someday.)

Refrain

This is the life.

Now I'm not sayin' that I never had a bad
    day.
But since I've been livin', livin' for Jesus,
Oh, this is what I have to say.

Refrain Twice

This is the life.

Refrain Twice

This is the life.
This is the life, y'all.
This is the life.

This Is Your Time

Words and Music by Michael W. Smith and Wes King

recorded by Michael W. Smith

It was a test we could all hope to pass,
But none of us would want to take.
Faced with the choice to deny God and live,
For her there was one choice to make.

Refrain 1:
This was her time, this was her dance,
She lived ev'ry moment, left nothin' to
    chance.
She swam in the sea, drank of the deep,
Embraced the mystery of all she could be;

This was her time.

Though you are mourning and grieving
    your loss,
Death died a long time ago.
Swallowed in life, so her life carries on,
Still, it's so hard to let go.

Refrain 1

What if tomorrow, and what if today
Faced with the question, oh, what would
    you say?

Refrain 2:
This is your time, this is your dance,
Live ev'ry moment, leave nothin' to chance.
To swim in the sea, drink of the deep,

And fall on the mercy and hear yourself
    praying,
"Won't You save me?
Won't You save me?"

Refrain 2

Embrace the mystery of all you can be.

Refrain 2

Embrace the mystery of all you can be.
This is your time.

Repeat and Fade:
Won't You save me?

This Mystery

Words and Music by Nichole Nordeman

recorded by Nichole Nordeman

Say goodnight to the light of the setting sun.
One more day, one more way of keeping track of all I've done.
I run this race, keep this pace, I'm doing fine.
And I won't stop until each box gets checked a second time.

And life becomes the 'round and 'round
Revolving door that won't slow down.
It won't slow down.

Refrain:
Do You wish, do You want us to breathe again?
Say goodbye to the lines that we've colored in
Brown and gray from day to day.
Oh, do You cry, do You hope for all things made new?
Try and try to invoke us to live in You
That we might be the hands and feet of this mystery.

This routine is nice and clean from dawn to dusk.
I rise and rest, I do my best.
When will it ever be enough?

And life becomes the bigger noise
Drowning out Your little voice,
Your little voice, Jesus.

Refrain

We take stock and we punch the clock
And we make sure all those zeroes are balanced in the end.

Refrain

That we might be the hands and feet,
That we might be the hands and feet of this mystery.
Yeah, this mystery.

Thy Word

Words and Music by Michael W. Smith and Amy Grant

recorded by Amy Grant

Refrain 1:
Thy Word is a lamp unto my feet
And a light unto my path.
Thy Word is a lamp unto my feet
And a light unto my path.

When I feel afraid,
Think I've lost my way,
Still You're there right beside me.
And—

Refrain 2:
Nothing will I fear
As long as You are near.
Please be near me to the end.

Refrain 1

Now I will not forget
Your love for me and yet
My heart forever is wandering.

Jesus, be my guide
And hold me to Your side,
And I will love You to the end.

Refrain 2

Refrain 1

And a light unto my path.
You're a light unto my path.

To Know You

Words and Music by Nichole Nordeman and Mark Hammond

recorded by Nichole Nordeman

It's well past midnight
And I'm awake with questions that won't
    wait for daylight,
Separating fact from my imaginary fiction
    on this shelf of my conviction.
I need to find a place where You and I
    come face to face.

Thomas needed proof that You had really
    risen undefeated.
When he placed his fingers where the nails
    once broke Your skin,
Did his faith fin'lly begin?
I've lied if I've denied the common ground
    I've shared with him.
And—

Refrain 1:
I really want to know You.
I want to make each day a diff'rent way
That I can show You how

Refrain 2:
I really wanted to love You.
Be patient with my doubt;
I'm just trying to figure out Your will,
And I really want to know You still.

Nicodemus could not understand how You
    could truly free us.
He struggled with the image of a grown man
    born again.
We might have been good friends,
'Cuz sometimes I still question, too, how eas-
    ily we come to You.
But—

Refrain 1

Refrain 2

No more campin' on the porch of indecision,
No more sleepin' under stars of apathy.
And it might be easier to dream, but
    dreamin's not for me.
And—

Refrain 1

I'm really gonna love You.
Be patient with my doubt;
I'm just trying to figure out Your will,
And I really want to know You still.

I want to know You.
Really want to know You.
Hey, hey—
I really want to know You.
I really want to know You.

True North

Words and Music by Twila Paris

recorded by Twila Paris

We lost our bearings following our own
   mind.
We left conviction behind.
Fear of the future springing from sins of
   the past,
Hiding the hope that would last.

How did we ever wander so far?
And where do we go from here?
How will we know where it is?

Refrain 1:
True north, there's a strong, steady light
   that is guiding us home.
True north, in the lingering night we were
   never alone.

True north.

Wonders of nature speak to us all of Your
   plan.
Why would we run from Your hand?
Laws of the earth, just like the laws of the
   heart,
Only begin where You are.

How did we ever wander so far?
And where do we go from here?
How will we find it again?

Refrain 1

Refrain 2:
We need an absolute compass now more
   than ever before.
True north.
(Keep shining the light, keep showing
   the way.)
True north.
(Star in the night, bright as the day.)

Turning back to where You meet us,
We will follow where You lead us.
There is truth inside Your dwelling.
We have come to face—

Refrain 1

Refrain 2

Dear Lord.
(Keep shining the light, keep showing
   the way.)
True north.
(Star in the night, bright as the day.)

Repeat and Fade:
Keep shining the light, keep showing the way.
Star in the night, bright as the day.

Trust His Heart

Words and Music by Eddie Carswell and Babbie Mason

recorded by Newsong; Cynthia Clawson & Wayne Watson

All things work for our good,
Though sometimes we can't see how they could.
Struggles that break our hearts in two
Sometimes blind us to the truth.

Our Father knows what's best for us;
His ways are not our own.
So when your pathway grows dim,
And you just can't see Him
Remember, you're never alone

Refrain:
God is too wise to be mistaken.
God is too good to be unkind.
So when you don't understand,
When you don't see His plan,
When you can't trace His hand,
Trust His heart.

He sees the master plan.
He holds the future in His hands.
So don't live as those who have no hope;
All our hope is found in Him.

We see the present clearly,
But He sees the first and the last.
And like a tapestry,
He's weaving you and me
To someday be just like Him.

Refrain

He alone is faithful and true.
He alone knows what is best for you.

Refrain

Undivided

Words and Music by Melodie Tunney

recorded by First Call

We may worship
Diff'rent ways.
We may praise Him,
And yet spend all of our days
Living life divided, divided.

But when we seek Him
With open hearts,
He removes the walls we've built
To keep us apart.
We trust Him to unite us.

Refrain:
In our hearts we're undivided,
Worshipping one Savior,
One Lord.
In our hearts we're undivided,
Bound by His spirit forever more,
Undivided.

It doesn't matter
If we agree.
All He asks is that
We serve Him faithfully
And love as He first loved us.

He made us in His image
And in His eyes we are all the same.
Though our methods may be diff'rent,
Jesus is the bond that will remain.

Refrain

In our hearts we're undivided.

Undo Me

Words and Music by Jennifer Knapp

recorded by Jennifer Knapp

Papa, I think I messed up again.
Was it something I did?
Was it somethin' I said?
I don't mean to do you wrong, it's just the
way of human nature,

Sister, I know I let you down.
I can tell by the fact you're never comin'
'round.
You don't have to say a thing;
I can tell by your eyes, exactly what you
mean.
That it's—

Refrain:
Time to get down on my knees and pray.
"Lord, undo me!
Put away my flesh and bone
'Til You own this spirit through me.
Lord,

Undo, me!"

Mama, I know I made you cry,
But I never meant to hurt you.
I never meant to lie.
While the world shook its head in shame,
I let you take the blame.

Brother, I know you labored so hard to
please,
Yeah, yeah, yeah.
But I cut you down, and I left you on your
knees.
Well, I know it must be, yeah—

Refrain

I am wanting, needing, guilty and greedy.
Unrighteous, unholy.
Undo me, undo me.

Abba Father, you must wonder why.
More times than Peter I have denied.
Three nails and a cross to prove
I owe my life eternally to you.
Well, it's time—

Refrain

Undo me.

Via Dolorosa

Words and Music by Billy Sprague and Niles Borop

recorded by Sandi Patty

Down the Via Dolorosa in Jerusalem that day,
The soldiers tried to clear the narrow street,
But the crowd pressed in to see
The man condemned to die on Calvary.

He was bleeding from a beating
There were stripes upon His back,
And He wore a crown of thorns upon His head;
And he bore with ev'ry step the scorn
Of those who cried out for His death.
Down the—

Refrain:
Via Dolorosa,
Called "The Way of Suffering,"
Like a lamb came the Messiah,
Christ the King.
But He chose to walk that road
Out of His love for you and me;
Down the Via Dolorosa,
All the way to Calvary.

The blood that would cleanse
The hearts of all men
Made its way through the heart
Of Jerusalem.
Down the—

Refrain

Wait for Me

Words and Music by Rebecca St. James

recorded by Rebecca St. James

Darling did you know that I, I dream about you?
Waiting for the look in your eyes
When we meet for the first time.
Darling, did you know that I, I pray about you?
Praying that you will hold on.
Keep your loving eyes only for me.

Refrain:
'Cause I am waiting for, praying for you, darling.
Wait for me, too.
Wait for me as I wait for you.
'Cause I am waiting for, praying for you, darling.
Wait for me, too.
Wait for me as I wait for you.
Darling wait; darling wait.

Darling, did you know I dream about life together,
Knowing it will be forever?
I'll be yours and you'll be mine.
And darling, when I say, "'Til death do us part,"
I'll mean it with all of my heart.
Now and always faithful to you.

Refrain

Now, I know you may have made mistakes,
But there's forgiveness and a second chance.
So wait for me, darling, wait for me.
Wait for me, wait for me.

Refrain Twice

Wait for me; darling, wait.
'Cause I'm waiting for you.
'Cause I'm waiting for you.
So wait for me.
Darling wait; wait for me.

The Warrior Is a Child

Words and Music by Twila Paris

recorded by Twila Paris

Lately I've been winning battles left and right.
But even winners can get wounded in the fight.
People say that I'm amazing, strong beyond my years.
But they don't see inside of me I'm hiding all the tears.

Refrain:
They don't know that I go running home when I fall down.
They don't know who picks me up when no one is around.
I drop my sword and cry for just a while,
'Cause deep inside this armor the warrior is a child.

Unafraid because His armor is the best.
But even soldiers need a quiet place to rest.
People say that I'm amazing, never face retreat.
But they don't see the enemies that lay me at His feet.

Refrain

They don't know that I go running home when I fall down.
They don't know who picks me up when no one is around.
I drop my sword and look up for a smile,
'Cause deep inside this armor,
Deep inside, deep inside this armor,
Deep inside this armor, deep inside this armor,
Deep inside this armor, the warrior is a child.

La la la…

The warrior is a child.

We Can Make a Difference

Words and Music by Mark Heimermann and David Mullen

recorded by Jaci Velasquez

Do do doot…

Come on, now.

We live in a dream
If we really think ev'rything's alright, yeah.
This world is in need, crying out to be freed,
We gotta shed some light, oh.

Refrain 1:
Teach the world to smile and hear
   angels sing;
Feel the breath of God and the pow'r
   it brings,
It's time to come together, you and I
And share the love of Jesus Christ.

Refrain 2:
We can make a diff'rence, we can make a
   change.
We can make the world a better place.
We can make a diff'rence, we can make a
   change.
We can make the sun shine through the rain,

Shine on through the rain.

Do do doot…

Do you know a man who's needing a hand?
Don't ya walk on by, oh.
A sister is sad, lost all that she had,
We gotta take the time, oh.
Look around your world, it will testify.
Some have empty hearts, some have
   hungry eyes.
God can heal the suff'ring through our
   hands.
Find compassion, take a stand.

Refrain 2

Shine on through the rain.

Do do doot…

Refrain 1

Refrain 2

Shine on through the rain.

Refrain 2

We can make a diff'rence, diff'rence,
   diff'rence, yeah.

Watch the Lamb

Words and Music by Ray Boltz

recorded by Ray Boltz

Walking on the road to Jerusalem,
The time had come to sacrifice again.
My two small sons, they walked beside me on the road.
The reason that they came was to watch the lamb.

"Daddy, Daddy, what will we see there?
There's so much that we don't understand."
So I told them of Moses and Father Abraham,
And then said, "Dear children, watch the lamb.

For there will be so many in Jerusalem today,
We must be sure the lamb doesn't run away."
Then I told them of Moses and Father Abraham,
And then I said "Dear children, watch the lamb."

And when we reached the city, I knew something must be wrong;
There were no joyful worshippers, no joyful worship songs.
I stood there with my children in the midst of angry men,
And then I heard the crowd cry out, "Crucify Him!"

We tried to leave the city, but we could not get away;
Forced to play in this drama, a part I did not wish to play.
Why upon this day were men condemned to die?
Why were we standing here where soon they would pass by?

I looked and said, "Even now they come."
The first one cried for mercy; the people gave him none.
The second one was violent, he was arrogant and loud.
I still hear his angry voice screaming at the crowd.

Then someone said, "There's Jesus!" and I scarce believed my eyes;
A man so badly beaten, He barely looked alive.
Blood poured from His body from the thorns upon His brow,
Running down the cross and falling to the ground.

I watched Him as He struggled, I watched Him as He fell.
The cross came down upon His back, the crowd began to yell.
In that moment I felt such agony; in that moment I felt such loss.
Until a Roman soldier grabbed my arm and screamed, "You carry His cross!"

At first I tried to resist him, then his hand reached for his sword;
And so I knelt and took the cross from the Lord.
I placed it on my shoulder and started down the street;
The blood that He'd been shedding was running down my cheek.

They led us to Golgotha, they drove nails deep in His feet and hands;
And yet upon the cross I heard Him pray, "Father, forgive them."
Oh, never have I seen such love in any other eyes.
"Into Thy hands I commit My Spirit," He prayed, and then He died.

I stood for what seemed like years, I'd lost all sense of time
Until I felt two tiny hands holding tight to mine.
My children stood there weeping; I heard the oldest say,
"Father, please forgive us, the lamb ran away.

Daddy, Daddy, What have we seen here?
There's so much that we don't understand."
So, I took them in my arms and we turned and faced the cross,
And then I said, "Dear children, watch the Lamb."

We Need Jesus

By John Elefante, Dino Elefante and Scott Springer

recorded by Petra with John Elefante & Lou Gramm

Verse 1:
When will the world see that we need Jesus?
If we open our eyes we will all realize that He loves us.
When will the world see that we need Jesus?
When our hearts are as one,
And believe that He's the Son of our God.

Refrain:
The Lord is our God,
And we shall never want.
The Lord is our God,
And we shall live forever.
When we share the love of Jesus,
See each other as He sees us,
Then His love will see us through,
His love will see us through.

Verse 2:
When will the world see that we need Jesus?
When sister and brother love one another as one.
When will the world see that we need Jesus?
Will we ever understand Jesus is the Son of man?
We must live in the shadow of His love.

Repeat Verses 1 and 2 and Fade

We Trust in the Name of the Lord Our God

Words and Music by Steven Curtis Chapman

recorded by Steve Green

Some trust in chariots;
We trust in the name of the Lord our God.
Some trust in horses;
We trust in the name of the Lord our God.

Refrain 1:
We trust in the name of the Lord our God.
We trust in the name of the Lord our God.
His love never fails,
His name will always prevail.

We trust in the name of the Lord our God.

Some trust in the work they do;
We trust in the name of the Lord our God.
'Cause by His grace all the work is through;
We trust in the name of the Lord our God.

Refrain 1

We trust in the name of the Lord our God.

Oh, glory to the name,
The name of our salvation.
Oh, glory to the name above all names,
The name of the Lord our God.
Some trust in the wealth of things;
We trust in the name of the Lord our God.
The name worth more than anything;
We trust in the name of the Lord our God.

Refrain 1

We trust in the name of the Lord our God.

Refrain 1

We trust in the name of the Lord our,
We trust in the name of the Lord our,
We trust in the name of the Lord our God.

Repeat Four Times:
Trust in the name, trust in the name, trust in
   the name.
Ah, trust in the name, trust in the name.
Trust in the name,

Name!

What Matters Most

Words and Music by Cheri Keaggy

recorded by Cheri Keaggy

Filling this verse with superlative words,
Making the most clever rhymes wouldn't amount to much,
Just wouldn't count for much if you can't read between the lines
But I have discovered, I've fin'lly uncovered
A most significant thing.
It's a noble theme.

Refrain:
What matters most is how much we love.
What matters most is how much we give.
What would it matter if we just lived without loving our God,
Without loving each other?

Faith, hope and love, especially love.
That's what matters most.
What matters most.

Once just a girl in a curious world, learning the meaning of life,
Tell me, what is the reason and why do the seasons
Keep turning the pages of time?
I had to discover the things from above,
For the days turn so quickly to years.
Then they disappear.

Refrain

Oh, not money, not power, not fame or position.
Don't want it, don't need it, don't give me religion.
All I wanna hear, all I wanna see, all I wanna read about is…
All I wanna live, all I wanna know, all I wanna be about is love.

What matters most.
Givin' love:
What matters most.

Refrain

What matters most is how much we love,
Setting our sights on the needs of our brother,
Loving our neighbor as we love ourselves.
We give to the Lord when we give to each other.

Faith, hope and love, especially love.
Faith, hope and love, especially love.
That's what matters most.
What matters most.

Repeat and Fade:
Faith, hope and love, especially love.

When God's People Pray

Words and Music by Wayne Watson

recorded by Wayne Watson

Trouble knocking on your windowpane,
Stormy weather at your door,
And the outlook for the day ahead
Like the day before.
People tell you praying changes things,
But words don't stop the fear.
A prayer is only pious rambling
Without the Father's ear.

He will not turn away when His people pray.

Refrain:
When God's people pray and take the pains
    of the earth
To the doors of heaven.
When God's people pray there is hope
    reborn,
There is sin forgiven,
And miracles you can't explain away.

When God's people pray.

Hopeless situation turns around,
Dilemma passes by and by.
Look, there's a never-ending field of blue
Past your clouded sky.
He alone can know the need in me
Before a single word begins.
The Holy Spirit intercedes for me,
I will trust in Him.

He will not turn away when His people pray.

Refrain

When God's people pray.
Oh, when God's people pray.
When God's people pray.

When I Consider

Words and Music by Wendi Foy Green and Carolyn Arends

recorded by Sierra

When I consider Your tenderness,
I am reminded of this:
Whenever I fail,
Your grace will prevail.
I know You love me no less,
When I consider Your tenderness.

When I consider Your righteousness,
I am reminded of this:
That I don't deserve
This love of such worth.
I know Your mercy exists,
When I consider Your righteousness.

When I consider Your faithfulness,
I am reminded of this:
When my strength is gone,
You carry me on.
I know in You I can rest,
When I consider Your faithfulness.

When I look deep into Your eyes of love,
When I remember the price that You paid,
When I consider all that You are,
All else fades away.

When I consider Your holiness,
I am reminded of this:
You're calling me to surrender to You.
I know I cannot resist,
When I consider Your holiness.
When I consider Your holiness.

When It's Time to Go

Words and Music by Jeff Silvey and Billy Simon

recorded by 4HIM

Nothing new in this old town,
The sun comes up and heads back down.
Working hard from dawn to dusk again.
Seventeen and a heart for a change,
The bi-ways calling out his name
But not yet; there's too much goin' on.

'Cause daddy needs a hand
And mama's tender heart might crumble to
    the ground.
Though they'd understand, he felt like
    saying

Refrain:
When it's time to go,
You've got to let me go away and face the
    world.
Say goodbye.
Cry some tears, don't worry.
When I hit the city I'll build you a house
Right down the street from mine.
Have some faith in me and I'll show you why.

Some years later late one night
He came in tryin' to dry his eyes;
He realized what he was born to do.
He said "I'll always be your son
And I know you know what's goin' on.
It's the hardest thing to think of leavin' you.

But this world needs a hand
And I've got just the thing they need to
    make it through.
It's so clear to me though I know what's
    coming.

Refrain

And as they tore His flesh like animals,
There were those I know who felt Him say:

Refrain Three Times

Where There Is Faith

Words and Music by Billy Simon

recorded by 4HIM

I believe in faithfulness, I believe in giving of myself
For someone else.
I believe in peace and love, I believe in honesty and trust.
But it's not enough;
For all that I believe may never change the way it is
Unless I believe that Jesus lives.

Refrain:
Where there is faith there is a voice calling;
Keep walking, you're not alone in this world.
Where there is faith there is a peace like a child sleeping,
Hope everlasting in He who is able to bear ev'ry burden,
To heal ev'ry hurt in my heart.
It is a wonderful, powerful place where there is faith.

There's a man across the sea never heard the sound of freedom ring,
Only in his dreams.
There's a lady dressed in black, in a motorcade of Cadillacs.
Daddy's not coming back.
Our hearts begin to fall and our stability grows weak,
But Jesus meets our needs.
If only we believe.

Refrain

Oh, where there is faith.
Oh, oh, oh, where there is faith.
Oh, oh.

Refrain

Where there is faith.

Why

Words and Music by Michael Card

recorded by Michael Card

Why did it have to be a friend
Who chose to betray the Lord?
And why did he use a kiss to show them?
That's not what a kiss is for.

Only a friend can betray a friend;
A stranger has nothing to gain.
And only a friend comes close enough
To ever cause so much pain.

And why did there have to be a thorny crown
Pressed upon His head?
It should have been a royal one
Made of jewels and gold instead.

It had to be a crown of thorns
Because in this life that we live,
For all who would seek to love,
A thorn is all the world has to give.

And why did there have to be a heavy cross
He was made to bear?
And why did they nail His feet and hands
When His love would have held Him there?

It was a cross, for on a cross a thief was supposed to pay;
And Jesus had come into the world
To steal ev'ry heart away,
Yes, Jesus had come into the world
To steal ev'ry heart away.

Wisdom

Words and Music by Twila Paris

recorded by Twila Paris

I see a multitude of people,
Some far away and some close by.
They weave together new religion
From tiny remnants they have found,
A bit of truth, a greater lie.
And all the prophets stand
And sing a pleasant song,
A million cords that bind
The spirit growing strong.
My heart is breaking, I must remind them:

Refrain:
You are the only way,
You are the only voice,
You are the only hope,
You are the only choice.
You are the one true God,
No matter what we say.
You are the breath of life,

You are the only way.
Give us wisdom.
Give us wisdom.

There is a moment of decision,
But all the days go rushing by,
An undercurrent of confusion
To threaten all that we believe
With little time to wonder why.
And all the prophets sing
The same familiar song;
Even the chosen can be led to sing along.
These hearts are breaking, will
   You remind us?

Refrain

You are the only way.
Give us wisdom.
Give us wisdom.

You chose the simple things to overcome the
   wise.
Wisdom is granted in the name of Jesus
   Christ.
In the name of Jesus Christ.

Refrain

We need You here today.
You are the only way.

Refrain

You are the only way.
Give us wisdom.
Give us wisdom.

Wise Up

Words and Music by Billy Simon and Wayne Kirkpatrick

recorded by Amy Grant

Got myself in this situation I'm not
    sure about,
Climbin' in where there's temptation.
Can I get back out?

Never can quite find the answer, the one I
    want to hear,
The one that justifies my actions, says the
    coast is clear.
Something on the outside says to jump on in,
Something on the inside is telling me again;

Refrain 1:
Better wise up, better think twice,
Never leave room for compromise.
Better wise up, better get smart,
Use your head to guard your heart.
It's gonna get rough,

So ya better wise up.

Take a look at your intentions, when you
    have to choose,
Could it be that apprehension might be
    tellin' you to

Refrain 2:
Back off now is better.
So, take your heart and run,
But get your thoughts together
Before they come undone;

Refrain 1

Refrain 3:
You've got to wise up,
You've got to think twice,
You've got to wise up,
You've got to, you've got to

Refrain 2

Refrain 1 Twice

Refrain 3 Twice

With a Little Faith

Words and Music by Lisa Kimmey, Michael Quinlan and David Wyatt

recorded by Stacie Orrico

I'd say I'm always happy if you want me to
But sometimes it's not the case.
My life's not as perfect as it seems to be;
It's simply God's amazing grace.

(I'm here to fin'lly let you know)
What keeps me hanging on,
What keeps me going strong.
(I'm here to share His love with you.)
There is no need to fear
To live His life of love.

Refrain:
With a little faith, with a little love,
I know we can make it.
I know we can make it
With a little help sent from God above.
I know we can make it, I know we can
    make it

Through.

Oh, I know what it takes to be yourself
Instead of when they put you down.
I can't understand why you choose to hide
When you should run to the strength I've
    found.

(If only you'd see for yourself,)
Then you could know the One
Who loves you so much more.

(If only I could help you out,)
But God's the only One.
What are you waiting for?

Refrain Twice

(It seems to wash away,)
Can't find a will to go on.
(But I am here to say.)
There's hope.
You must carry on.
(Jesus will light your way,)
He'll give you all that you need.
(No need to be afraid.)
All you've got to do is believe.

Refrain Twice

Through.

(With a little, with a little, yeah.)

With All My Heart

Words and Music by Babbie Mason

recorded by Babbie Mason

In this quiet place with You,
I bow before Your throne.
I bare the deepest part of me
To You and You alone.
I keep no secrets,
For there is no thought
You have not known.
I bring my best, and all the rest,
To You and lay them down.

Refrain:
With all my heart
I want to love You, Lord.
And live my life
Each day to know You more.
All that is in me
Is Yours completely.
I'll serve You only,
With all my heart.

You faithfully supply my needs
According to Your plan.
So help me, Lord,
To seek Your face
Before I seek Your hand.
And trust You know what's best for me
When I don't understand.
Then follow in obedience
In ev'ry circumstance.

Refrain

Wonder Why

Words and Music by Grant Cunningham and Matt Huesmann

recorded by Avalon

Male:
Why, why?
Tell me, do you wonder why
Some can look so hard and miss the truth?
Some will stumble over it a hundred times
And never ever see the living proof.

Well, there's a kind of love the world could
 never deny.
Let ev'rybody see it in our lives.

Refrain:
The world will wonder why
If you and I will shine His light.
And hearts discover life
When we decide to let ours go.
We've got to give it up
And live the love that opened our eyes.
Live your life.
The world will wonder why.

Yeah…will wonder why.

Female:
Why, why?
Someone try and tell me why
We would want it any other way?
A heart could change before our very eyes.
Well, I've seen the diff'rence that love can
 make.

Where is the kind of love this world could
 never explain?
It's time to live the Gospel unashamed.

Refrain

Oh, yes they will.

Group:
If we were living with a passion,
What would be the reaction?
If we were loving with a strong love,
Then their eyes would see
And the world might believe.
The world will wonder why.
Wonder why.

Refrain

If we shine the light,
If we live our life they will wonder why.

Refrain

Would I Know You

Words and Music by Wayne Watson

recorded by Wayne Watson

Would I know You now if You walked into the room,
If You stilled the crowd, if Your light dispelled the gloom?
And if I saw Your wounds, touched Your thorn-pierced brow,
I wonder if I'd know You now.

Would I know You now if You walked into this place?
Would I cause You shame, would my games be Your disgrace?
Or would I worship You, fall upon my face?
I wonder if I'd know You now.

Or have the images I've painted so distorted who You are
That even if the world was looking, they could not see You;
The real You?
Have I changed the true reflection to fulfill my own design,
Making You what I want, not showing You forth divine,
Divine?

Would I miss You now if You left and closed the door?
Would my flesh cry out, "I don't need You anymore!"
Or would I follow You, could I be restored?
I wonder, I wonder, will I ever learn?
I wonder, would I know You now?

Your Grace Still Amazes Me

Words and Music by Shawn Craig and Connie Harrington

recorded by Phillips, Craig & Dean

My faithful Father, enduring Friend.
Your tender mercy's like a river with no end.

It overwhelms me, covers my sin.
Each time I come into Your presence
I stand in wonder once again.

Refrain:
Your grace still amazes me,
Your love is still a mystery.
Each day I fall on my knees,
'Cause Your grace still amazes me.
Your grace still amazes me.

Oh, patient Savior, You make me whole.
You are the Author and the Healer of my soul.

What can I give You, Lord, what can I say?
I know there's no way to repay You,
Only to offer You my praise.

Refrain

It's deeper, it's wider,
It's stronger, it's higher.
It's deeper, it's wider,
It's stronger than anything my eyes can see.

Refrain

Artist Index

Songwriter Index

Toby McKeehan
11 Always Have, Always Will
19 Between You and Me
28 Colored People
31 Consume Me
107 Into Jesus
110 Jesus Freak
152 My Will

Douglas McKelvey
26 Circle of Friends

Steve Millikan
78 Heaven Is Counting on You
98 I Think I See Gold

David Moffitt
97 I Surrender All

Jon Mohr
143 The Mission

Geoff Moore
53 For Who He Really Is
68 The Great Adventure
123 Listen to Our Hearts
125 Live Out Loud
178 Speechless

Cindy Morgan
88 How Could I Ask for More
99 I Will Be Free
184 Take My Life

Dan Muckala
72 He Walked a Mile

David Mullen
201 We Can Make a Difference

Rich Mullins
17 Awesome God
40 Doubly Good to You
82 Hold Me Jesus
132 Love of Another Kind
173 Sing Your Praise to the Lord

Phil Naish
145 More to This Life

Greg Nelson
160 People Need the Lord

Nichole Nordeman
45 Every Season
51 Fool for You
191 This Mystery
193 To Know You

Michael Omartian
135 Lover of My Soul
141 The Message

Stacie Orrico
38 Don't Look at Me

Twila Paris
44 Every Heart That Is Breaking
47 Faithful Friend
61 God Is in Control
87 How Beautiful
113 The Joy of the Lord
120 Lamb of God
150 My Utmost for His Highest
165 Run to You
194 True North
200 The Warrior Is a Child
213 Wisdom

Charlie Peacock
106 In the Light
138 A Maze of Grace
166 Say the Name

Daniel Pitts
152 My Will

Henk Pool
185 Testify to Love

Otto Price
8 Abba (Father)

Joe Priolo
14 Anything Is Possible
126 Living for You

Michael Quinlan
164 Pray
215 With a Little Faith

Chris Rice
58 Go Light Your World

Robert Riekerk
185 Testify to Love

John Rosasco
86 Household of Faith

Gary Sadler
163 Pour My Love on You

Rebecca St. James
8 Abba (Father)
39 Don't Worry
57 Go and Sin No More
59 God
142 Mirror
164 Pray
180 Stand
199 Wait for Me

Jerry Salley
81 His Strength Is Perfect

Steve Siler
26 Circle of Friends

Jeff Silvey
210 When It's Time to Go

Billy Simon
137 A Man You Would Write About
210 When It's Time to Go
211 Where There Is Faith
214 Wise Up

Tower Sloan
183 Stubborn Love

Deborah D. Smith
32 Could He Be the Messiah
55 Friends
71 Great Is the Lord
84 Hosanna
172 Shine on Us

Martin Smith
35 Deeper
46 Everything
66 God's Romance

Michael W. Smith
12 Angels
16 Arms of Love
32 Could He Be the Messiah
34 Cross of Gold
50 Find a Way
55 Friends
56 Give It Away
62 God of All of Me
71 Great Is the Lord
84 Hosanna
91 How Majestic Is Your Name
93 I Am Sure
103 I'll Lead You Home
133 Love One Another
162 Place in This World
168 Secret Ambition
172 Shine on Us
183 Stubborn Love
190 This Is Your Time
192 Thy Word

Paul Smith
90 How Excellent Is Thy Name

Scotty Smith
129 Lord of the Dance

Billy Sprague
198 Via Dolorosa

Scott Springer
204 We Need Jesus

Robert Sterling
109 Jesus Will Still Be There

More Collections from The Lyric Library

BROADWAY VOLUME I

An invaluable collection of lyrics to 200 top Broadway tunes, including: All at Once You Love Her • All I Ask of You • And All That Jazz • Any Dream Will Do • As Long As He Needs Me • At the End of the Day • Autumn in New York • Bali Ha'i • Bewitched • Cabaret • Castle on a Cloud • Climb Ev'ry Mountain • Comedy Tonight • Don't Rain on My Parade • Everything's Coming up Roses • Hello, Dolly! • I Could Have Danced All Night • I Dreamed a Dream • I Remember It Well • If I Were a Bell • It's the Hard-Knock Life • Let Me Entertain You • Mame • My Funny Valentine • Oklahoma • Seasons of Love • September Song • Seventy Six Trombones • Shall We Dance? • Springtime for Hitler • Summer Nights • Tomorrow • Try to Remember • Unexpected Song • What I Did for Love • With One Look • You'll Never Walk Alone • (I Wonder Why?) You're Just in Love • and more.

_____00240201 ....$14.95

BROADWAY VOLUME II

200 more favorite Broadway lyrics (with no duplication from Volume I): Ain't Misbehavin' • All of You • Another Op'nin', Another Show • As If We Never Said Goodbye • Beauty School Dropout • The Best of Times • Bring Him Home • Brotherhood of Man • Camelot • Close Every Door • Consider Yourself • Do-Re-Mi • Edelweiss • Getting to Know You • Have You Met Miss Jones? • I Loved You Once in Silence • I'm Flying • If Ever I Would Leave You • The Impossible Dream (The Quest) • It Only Takes a Moment • The Lady Is a Tramp • The Last Night of the World • A Little More Mascara • Lost in the Stars • Love Changes Everything • Me and My Girl • Memory • My Heart Belongs to Daddy • On a Clear Day (You Can See Forever) • On My Own • People • Satin Doll • The Sound of Music • Sun and Moon • The Surrey with the Fringe on Top • Unusual Way (In a Very Unusual Way) • We Kiss in a Shadow • We Need a Little Christmas • Who Will Buy? • Wishing You Were Somehow Here Again • Younger Than Springtime • and more.

_____00240205 ....$14.95

CHRISTMAS

200 lyrics to the most loved Christmas songs of all time, including: Angels We Have Heard on High • Auld Lang Syne • Away in a Manger • Baby, It's Cold Outside • The Chipmunk Song • The Christmas Shoes • The Christmas Song (Chestnuts Roasting on an Open Fire) • Christmas Time Is Here • Do They Know It's Christmas? • Do You Hear What I Hear • Feliz Navidad • The First Noel • Frosty the Snow Man • The Gift • God Rest Ye Merry, Gentlemen • Goin' on a Sleighride • Grandma Got Run over by a Reindeer • Happy Xmas (War Is Over) • He Is Born, the Holy Child (Il Est Ne, Le Divin Enfant) • The Holly and the Ivy • A Holly Jolly Christmas • (There's No Place Like) Home for the Holidays • I Heard the Bells on Christmas Day • I Wonder As I Wander • I'll Be Home for Christmas • I've Got My Love to Keep Me Warm • In the Bleak Midwinter • It Came upon the Midnight Clear • It's Beginning to Look like Christmas • It's Just Another New Year's Eve • Jingle Bells • Joy to the World • Mary, Did You Know? • Merry Christmas, Darling • The Most Wonderful Time of the Year • My Favorite Things • Rudolph the Red-Nosed Reindeer • Silent Night • Silver Bells • The Twelve Days of Christmas • What Child Is This? • What Made the Baby Cry? • Wonderful Christmastime • and more.

_____00240206 ....$14.95

See our website for a complete contents list for each volume:
www.halleonard.com

FOR MORE INFORMATION, SEE YOUR LOCAL MUSIC DEALER,
OR WRITE TO:

HAL•LEONARD®
CORPORATION
7777 W. BLUEMOUND RD. P.O. BOX 13819 MILWAUKEE, WI 53213

Prices, contents and availability subject to change without notice.

More Collections from The Lyric Library

CLASSIC ROCK

Lyrics to 200 essential rock classics songs, including: All Day and All of the Night • All Right Now • Angie • Another One Bites the Dust • Back in the U.S.S.R. • Ballroom Blitz • Barracuda • Beast of Burden • Bell Bottom Blues • Brain Damage • Brass in Pocket • Breakdown • Breathe • Bus Stop • California Girls • Carry on Wayward Son • Centerfold • Changes • Cocaine • Cold As Ice • Come Sail Away • Come Together • Crazy Little Thing Called Love • Crazy on You • Don't Do Me like That • Don't Fear the Reaper • Don't Let the Sun Go down on Me • Don't Stand So Close to Me • Dreamer • Drive My Car • Dust in the Wind • 867-5309/Jenny • Emotional Rescue • Every Breath You Take • Every Little Thing She Does Is Magic • Eye in the Sky • Eye of the Tiger • Fame • Forever Young • Fortress Around Your Heart • Free Ride • Give a Little Bit • Gloria • Godzilla • Green-Eyed Lady • Heartache Tonight • Heroes • Hey Joe • Hot Blooded • I Fought the Law • I Shot the Sheriff • I Won't Back Down • Instant Karma • Invisible Touch • It's Only Rock 'N' Roll (But I like It) • It's Still Rock and Roll to Me • Layla • The Logical Song • Long Cool Woman (In a Black Dress) • Love Hurts • Maggie May • Me and Bobby McGee • Message in a Bottle • Mississippi Queen • Money • Money for Nothing • My Generation • New Kid in Town • Nights in White Satin • Paradise by the Dashboard Light • Piano Man • Rebel, Rebel • Refugee • Rhiannon • Roxanne • Shattered • Smoke on the Water • Sultans of Swing • Sweet Emotion • Walk This Way • We Gotta Get Out of This Place • We Will Rock You • Wouldn't It Be Nice • and many more!

_____00240183 ....$14.95

CONTEMPORARY CHRISTIAN

An amazing collection of 200 lyrics from some of the most prominent Contemporary Christian artists: Abba (Father) • After the Rain • Angels • Awesome God • Breathe on Me • Circle of Friends • Doubly Good to You • Down on My Knees • El Shaddai • Father's Eyes • Friends • Give It Away • Go Light Your World • God's Own Fool • Grand Canyon • The Great Adventure • The Great Divide • He Walked a Mile • Heaven and Earth • Heaven in the Real World • His Strength Is Perfect • Household of Faith • How Beautiful • I Surrender All • Jesus Freak • Joy in the Journey • Judas' Kiss • A Little More • Live Out Loud • Love Will Be Our Home • A Maze of Grace • The Message • My Utmost for His Highest • Oh Lord, You're Beautiful • People Need the Lord • Pray • Say the Name • Signs of Life • Speechless • Stand • Steady On • Via Dolorosa • The Warrior Is a Child • What Matters Most • Would I Know You • and more.

_____00240184 ....$14.95

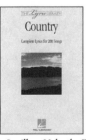

COUNTRY

A great resource of lyrics to 200 of the best country songs of all time, including: Act Naturally • All My Ex's Live in Texas • All the Gold in California • Always on My Mind • Amazed • American Made • Angel of the Morning • Big Bad John • Blue • Blue Eyes Crying in the Rain • Boot Scootin' Boogie • Breathe • By the Time I Get to Phoenix • Could I Have This Dance • Crazy • Daddy's Hands • D-I-V-O-R-C-E • Down at the Twist and Shout • Elvira • Folsom Prison Blues • Friends in Low Places • The Gambler • Grandpa (Tell Me 'Bout the Good Old Days) • Harper Valley P.T.A. • He Thinks He'll Keep Her • Hey, Good Lookin' • I Fall to Pieces • I Hope You Dance • I Love a Rainy Night • I Saw the Light • I've Got a Tiger by the Tail • Islands in the Stream • Jambalaya (On the Bayou) • The Keeper of the Stars • King of the Road • Lucille • Make the World Go Away • Mammas Don't Let Your Babies Grow up to Be Cowboys • My Baby Thinks He's a Train • Okie from Muskogee • Ring of Fire • Rocky Top • Sixteen Tons • Stand by Me • There's a Tear in My Beer • Walkin' After Midnight • When You Say Nothing at All • Where the Stars and Stripes and the Eagle Fly • Where Were You (When the World Stopped Turning) • You Are My Sunshine • Your Cheatin' Heart • and more.

_____00240204 ....$14.95

See our website for a complete contents list for each volume:
www.halleonard.com

FOR MORE INFORMATION, SEE YOUR LOCAL MUSIC DEALER,
OR WRITE TO:

HAL•LEONARD®
CORPORATION

7777 W. BLUEMOUND RD. P.O. BOX 13819 MILWAUKEE, WI 53213

Prices, contents and availability subject to change without notice.

More Collections from The Lyric Library

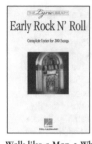

EARLY ROCK 'N' ROLL

Lyrics to 200 top songs that started the rock 'n' roll revolution, including: All I Have to Do Is Dream • All Shook Up • At the Hop • Baby Love • Barbara Ann • Be-Bop-A-Lula • Big Girls Don't Cry • Blue Suede Shoes • Bo Diddley • Book of Love • Calendar Girl • Chantilly Lace • Charlie Brown • Crying • Dancing in the Street • Do Wah Diddy Diddy • Don't Be Cruel (To a Heart That's True) • Earth Angel • Fun, Fun, Fun • Great Balls of Fire • He's a Rebel • Heatwave (Love Is like a Heatwave) • Hello Mary Lou • Hound Dog • I Walk the Line • It's My Party • Kansas City • The Loco-Motion • My Boyfriend's Back • My Guy • Oh, Pretty Woman • Peggy Sue • Rock and Roll Is Here to Stay • Sixteen Candles • Splish Splash • Stand by Me • Stupid Cupid • Surfin' U.S.A. • Teen Angel • A Teenager in Love • Twist and Shout • Walk like a Man • Where the Boys Are • Why Do Fools Fall in Love • Willie and the Hand Jive • and more.

_____00240203 ....$14.95

LOVE SONGS

Lyrics to 200 of the most romantic songs ever written, including: All My Loving • Always in My Heart (Siempre En Mi Corazon) • And I Love Her • Anniversary Song • Beautiful in My Eyes • Call Me Irresponsible • Can You Feel the Love Tonight • Cheek to Cheek • (They Long to Be) Close to You • Could I Have This Dance • Dedicated to the One I Love • Don't Know Much • Dream a Little Dream of Me • Endless Love • Fields of Gold • For Once in My Life • Grow Old with Me • The Hawaiian Wedding Song (Ke Kali Nei Au) • Heart and Soul • Hello, Young Lovers • How Deep Is the Ocean (How High Is the Sky) • I Just Called to Say I Love You • I'll Be There • I've Got My Love to Keep Me Warm • Just the Way You Are • Longer • L-O-V-E • Love Will Keep Us Together • Misty • Moonlight in Vermont • More (Ti Guardero' Nel Cuore) • My Funny Valentine • My Heart Will Go on (Love Theme from 'Titanic') • She • Speak Softly, Love (Love Theme) • Till • A Time for Us (Love Theme) • Unchained Melody • Up Where We Belong • We've Only Just Begun • What the World Needs Now Is Love • When I Fall in Love • Witchcraft • Wonderful Tonight • You Are the Sunshine of My Life • You're the Inspiration • You've Made Me So Very Happy • and more!

_____00240186 ....$14.95

POP/ROCK BALLADS

Lyrics to 200 top tunes of the pop/rock era, including: Adia • After the Love Has Gone • Against All Odds (Take a Look at Me Now) • Always on My Mind • Amazed • And So It Goes • Baby What a Big Surprise • Ben • Breathe • Change the World • Come to My Window • Do You Know Where You're Going To? • Don't Cry Out Loud • Don't Fall in Love with a Dreamer • Don't Let Me Be Lonely Tonight • Easy • Feelings (?Dime?) • Fire and Rain • From a Distance • Georgia on My Mind • Hero • I Hope You Dance • Imagine • In the Air Tonight • Iris • Just My Imagination (Running Away with Me) • Killing Me Softly with His Song • Laughter in the Rain • Looks like We Made It • My Heart Will Go on (Love Theme from 'Titanic') • New York State of Mind • The Rainbow Connection • Rainy Days and Mondays • Sailing • She's Always a Woman • Sing • Sunshine on My Shoulders • Take Me Home, Country Roads • Tears in Heaven • There You'll Be • Time After Time • Vision of Love • The Way We Were • Woman in Love • You're the Inspiration • You've Got a Friend • and more.

_____00240187 ....$14.95

See our website for a complete contents list for each volume:
www.halleonard.com

FOR MORE INFORMATION, SEE YOUR LOCAL MUSIC DEALER,
OR WRITE TO:

HAL•LEONARD®
CORPORATION

7777 W. BLUEMOUND RD. P.O. BOX 13819 MILWAUKEE, WI 53213

Prices, contents and availability subject to change without notice.